When God makes streams in the desert

Revival blessings in the Bible

Roger Ellsworth

DayOne

© Day One Publications 2009
First Edition 2009

British Library Cataloguing in Publication Data available

ISBN 978-1-84625-176-4

Published by Day One Publications
Ryelands Road, Leominster, HR6 8NZ

☎ 01568 613 740
FAX: 01568 611 473
email—sales@dayone.co.uk
web site—www.dayone.co.uk
North American e-mail—usasales@dayone.co.uk
North American web site—www.dayonebookstore.com

Designed by Wayne McMaster and printed by Gutenberg Press, Malta

This book is dedicated to my
good friend of many years,
David Clark

Endorsements

With a relentless focus on the Bible itself, Roger Ellsworth reminds us that true revival is a sovereign work of God that radically affects our lives. The best recommendation I can give of this book is that it made me long more intensely and pray more fervently for God to act in the midst of his people.

Chad Davis, Pastor, Grace Community Church, Martin, Tennessee, USA

'O LORD, I have heard Your speech and was afraid; O LORD, revive Your work in the midst of the years! In the midst of the years make it known' (Hab. 3:2). Roger Ellsworth creates a thirst in the heart for God to renew his works in our day. We live in a day when spiritual dryness and barrenness are so commonplace and widespread that they somehow seem normal. Like a man who has become accustomed to constant dehydration, we assume our symptoms are 'just the way it is'. We have forgotten that we are to have cups that overflow. With careful examination of the Word of God, When God Makes Streams in the Desert *reminds a parched church that there IS a fountain of renewal. The book has a refreshing accessibility that makes it readable for every Christian, and a depth that makes it imperative for every pastor.*

Revd Jason T. Hartig, Pastor, Smyrna Baptist Church, Humboldt, Tennessee, USA

When God Makes Streams in the Desert *reminds us that revival is present when, as Brian Edwards says, 'remarkable life and power that cannot be explained adequately in any human terms' moves into our churches and causes us to do what we do 'at a different level'. This book will change the way you think about and pray for revival.*

Paul Orrick, Pastor, First Baptist Church, Greenville, Ohio, USA

Acknowledgements

I count it a privilege to work with Jim Holmes and Day One to further the cause of biblical revival. How urgently we need it! May it come quickly!

I am also indebted to my wife Sylvia for dreaming with me about the possibility of revival and for working with me on these chapters.

Contents

Introduction

We are familiar with the words 'revive', 'revived' and 'revival'. When a sick person begins to improve after having been at death's door, it is not unusual to hear someone say that that individual has 'revived'. When an athlete's performance improves after a period of marked decline, a sports analyst might tell us that the player has experienced a revival.

To 'revive' something is to bring it back to life or vitality. To come back from a low, weak and moribund state is to experience 'revival'.

The word 'revival' is well known by Christians. The familiarity may be due to a custom that now appears to be dying out, that is, conducting revival meetings. For many years, evangelical churches would conduct one or two such meetings annually. They would bring in a guest preacher and guest singer and offer special evening services for a week or two. These meetings were designed to encourage believers to get closer to the Lord and to convince unbelievers to accept the Lord.

But revival is not a series of meetings. We can meet, meet and meet, yet never get anywhere near real revival. So while most Christians are familiar with the word 'revival', they do not always have a good grasp of its meaning.

'Revival' is God bringing his people back to spiritual vitality or life. It pertains only to Christians because only they have spiritual life, having been regenerated by the Spirit of God on the basis of the redeeming work of Christ. The whole problem with unbelievers is that they lack this life, being dead in their trespasses and sins (Eph. 2:1).

The fact that revival means Christians are brought back to life should not be construed to mean that they have lost their salvation and it is restored to them by revival. That cannot happen. Salvation is God's work, and it is a sure work (Phil. 1:6). We ourselves may sometimes describe a family member or friend as 'lifeless'. We do not mean that the person is dead but rather that he or she is lacking in energy and vigour, and Christians can become 'lifeless' in this sense. They are still alive spiritually, but they are lacking in spiritual vigour and energy. Revival restores them. It brings back the energy and vitality.

J. I. Packer calls revival the 'renewing [of] the inner life of Christians who have grown slack and sleepy'. He calls it the giving of 'new spiritual awareness to those whose hearts and consciences had been blind, hard and cold'.[1] Revival does not give Christians something new. It makes old things new.

We should also note that revival is not something that Christians can do for themselves. Christians did not save themselves, and they cannot revive themselves. Both are works of the sovereign God. Eifion Evans defines revival as '... God manifesting Himself in a sovereign, spontaneous, powerful and general manner, bringing about the quickening of spiritual life in His people and the conversion of the ungodly'.[2] Revival comes from God! We cannot predict it or produce it. Brian H. Edwards further writes, 'Revival is remarkable, large, effective, and, above all, it is something that *God* brings about. It is quite impossible for man to create revival. Though men may prepare and pray for it, revival is the work of the sovereign God, not primarily for the benefit of his people, but for his own honour and glory' (italics are his).[3]

The fact that revival is God's prerogative brings us face to face with a troublesome question: Why do we not see revival more often? Revival is obviously a good thing. So why does God not grant it more quickly and frequently?

The answer to that question is locked up in the same sovereignty that grants revival. The sovereignty that bestows revival decides when to bestow it. It is not ours to figure out why God acts as he does. It is rather ours to seek his face. The very fact that we are inclined to seek means that God is already at work.

In the pages that follow, we will look at the Bible's teachings on revival. We will do so, first, by laying a foundation for the doctrine of revival. We will then turn our attention to revival glory, that is, to some of the glorious things that revival accomplishes when it comes. In the final section, we will seek to fan the flame of expectation in our hearts for God's work of revival.

May the God of revival be pleased to use these pages to refine our understanding of revival and to ignite a passion to see it, and may that passion so burn in our hearts that each day we will find ourselves taking as our own the following petitions: 'Will you not revive us again, that Your people may rejoice in You? (Ps. 85:6); 'O LORD, revive Your work in the midst of the years! In the midst of the years make it known; in wrath remember mercy' (Hab. 3:2).

Revival foundation

God has a people

But you are a chosen generation, a royal priesthood, a holy nation, His own special people, that you may proclaim the praises of Him who called you out of darkness into His marvelous light;

Who once were not a people but are now the people of God, who had not obtained mercy but now have obtained mercy.

1 Peter 2:9–10

The starting place for this series of studies may seem a bit unusual. I hope it will make sense in time! I want us to begin with this basic affirmation: God has a people.

We often glide right past profound truth without truly savouring it. How easy it is for us to glide past this truth! How easy it is for us to miss the wonder of it! May God bring that wonder back to our minds and hearts as we consider the words of our text.

We can divide the apostle Peter's words into three parts: 'you were', 'you are' and 'that you'.

You were

The people of God have not always been the people of God! That flies in the face of modern thinking and teaching, which insists that we are automatically the people of God. Be a people, and you are among the people of God!

The apostle Peter adamantly rejects this notion, plainly telling his readers that they 'once were not a people' (v. 10).

The truth is that we do not come into this world as part of the people of God. On the contrary; we are by nature the people of Satan. We enter this world with a sinful nature that makes us part of Satan's domain. The apostle Paul puts it in these words: ' we … were by nature children of wrath, just as the others' (Eph. 2:3). In other words, each one of us is a sinner by nature!

Paul also tells us that we once were 'dead in trespasses and sins' (Eph. 2:1). When you are dead, there is nothing that you can do to help yourself. The only hope for dead sinners is for God in mercy to grant them spiritual life. Until that mercy comes, they are not among the people of God. To say, therefore, that we once were not among the people of God is also to say that there was a time when we had not received mercy, which, by the way, is exactly what the apostle Peter affirms (v. 10 of our text).

The apostle also tells his readers that they were once in darkness (v. 9). They were not naturally among the people of God, and they could not understand that they were not. They were in a bad condition, but they could not see their condition. The apostle Paul affirms that the minds of sinners have been blinded by Satan (2 Cor. 4:4).

You are

So Peter's readers were once in a most tragic and lamentable condition indeed, but they did not stay in that condition. God had come along, found them in their spiritual deadness and had granted them spiritual life. He had granted them the mercy they so desperately needed. They were not what they once were! They were radically different.

So different were they that Peter was able to describe them with these four phrases:

A CHOSEN GENERATION (OR RACE)

The readers of this letter were now among the people of God because God had chosen them to be so. This is the doctrine of election that is despised, neglected, abused and distorted. Some try to explain this doctrine in terms of God looking down through the corridor of time to see who will choose him, and then choosing them first! But people dead in their sins could not do such a thing! Dead people can't choose anything. Only the living can choose.

Sinners do choose God, but their choosing is the result of his choosing. God in mercy placed his heart on people in eternity past without any reference to merit in them. He chose them simply because it pleased him to do so. Those whom God chose are quickened, or made alive, by his Spirit. And then they gladly and freely choose the Lord.

It is not a matter of us choosing God. That would make him grateful to us. It is rather a matter of him choosing us and making us eternally grateful to him.

A ROYAL PRIESTHOOD

The people of God have been called out of the most terrible condition and elevated to the highest office. As priests, they now offer to God spiritual sacrifices (1 Peter 2:5). We offer to God our minds and bodies (Rom. 12:1–2) and our praises to his glory (Heb. 13:15–16).

A HOLY NATION

Israel was chosen by God to be his holy nation in the Old Testament. Now he has a new nation, consisting of all those whom he has chosen. This nation does not have physical boundaries; it transcends them, comprising people from every nation who own Jesus Christ as Lord.

GOD'S OWN SPECIAL PEOPLE

With this phrase, the apostle assured his readers of something incredibly glorious—God takes delight in his people. He regards them as his own special treasure. We may sometimes allow ourselves to think that we have no worth or value, that we are not special to anyone. But all God's people are special to him. He prizes them as his jewels (Mal. 3:17).

How could it be otherwise? These are people for whom God has paid an enormously high price. He purchased them for himself at the cost of the death of his Son, and that death was like no other. It was far more than physical death; Jesus actually endured the wrath of God in the place of sinners.

That you

Once not a people! Once without mercy! Once in darkness! Now a chosen generation, royal priesthood, holy nation and God's own special people! And all because of God's incredible mercy!

What should our response be to these things? The apostle Peter leaves no doubt. He writes, '... that you may proclaim the praises of Him who called you out of darkness into His marvelous light ...' (v. 9).

We are God's called people. The calling made all the difference! We have been called out of sin's domain to the high privilege of being God's people. How can we not praise him? The apostle Paul declares, 'For you were bought at a price; therefore glorify God in your body and in your spirit, which are God's' (1 Cor. 6:20).

What does it mean to live for his glory? It means to live in such a way that others can only explain us in terms of God having touched our lives. It means living in such a way that others will be made conscious of God, and God will get the credit for the obvious change that has been made in us.

God made man to live for his glory. Sin keeps us from doing that (Rom. 3:23). But God's people, redeemed from their sins, can now realize the high purpose for which they were made.

Reflect on these points

1. *We do not come into this world as part of the people of God. On the contrary; we are by nature the people of Satan.*

2. *It is not a matter of us choosing God. It is rather a matter of him choosing us and making us eternally grateful to him.*

3. *God takes delight in his people. All God's people are special to him. He prizes them as his jewels.*

4. *If we are God's called people, how can we not praise him?*

God has expectations for his people

And now, Israel, what does the LORD your God require of you, but to fear the LORD your God, to walk in all His ways and to love Him, to serve the LORD your God with all your heart and with all your soul,

And to keep the commandments of the LORD and His statutes which I command you today for your good?

Deuteronomy 10:12–13

We are beginning our study of the vital theme of revival by putting in place certain truths that could be called 'underpinnings' for the doctrine. The first of these was simply that God has a people. We now turn our attention to a second basic truth: God has certain expectations for his people. God has not called people to himself for no reason.

We could go to any one of several passages for guidance on this matter, but no passage puts it better than the one we have before us. Here we have Moses, the leader of the nation of Israel, preaching to his people. His preaching takes up most of the book of Deuteronomy, and our text is drawn from the second and longest of his three sermons that make up this book (4:44–28:68).

Moses addresses the matter of God's expectations for his people. He asks, 'And now, Israel, what does the LORD your God require of you ...?' (v. 12).

Does this have any application to us? Indeed it does. We have established that God has a people today. All who belong to God today through faith in the Lord Jesus Christ are part of God's new Israel, spiritual Israel. The true sons of Abraham are those who have the faith of Abraham (Rom. 2:28–29; 4:16;

Gal. 3:7–9). So this passage speaks to us with the same force that it did to those Israelites long ago. But what does it say? What does the Lord expect of his people?

We are to fear the Lord (v. 12)

The fear of the Lord consists of more than one element. It first means to stand in awe of his person. It can be defined as reverence for God which arises from a consciousness of his majesty and glory.

The Bible always emphasizes the majesty and splendour of God, which far surpass our ability to comprehend. Moses calls our attention to God's greatness with these words: 'Indeed heaven and the highest heavens belong to the LORD your God, also the earth with all that is in it' (Deut. 10:14).

God is unlimited in power and wisdom. He is the Creator of all things and the ruler and sustainer of all things. He is holy, completely without the taint of sin. The angels of heaven, awesome beings in their own right, stand in awe of God. How much more, then, should we!

But, sadly, the modern church seems allergic to reverence for God, often associating it with deadness and formalism. Of one thing we can be sure: when true revival comes, the people of God will not have to be told to reverence him!

Also bound up in the fear of the Lord is the dread of his displeasure. When the fear of the Lord is mentioned, someone inevitably says, 'I don't think that means that we should be afraid of God.' But this God does have expectations of his people, and he warns us of his chastisement if we refuse to heed those expectations. We would do well to be afraid of God's chastisement (Heb. 12:5–12).

As so often, Matthew Henry puts the matter perfectly by saying of the fear of God, 'We must adore his majesty, acknowledge his authority, stand in awe of his power, and dread his wrath.'[1]

We are to walk in all his ways (v. 12)

Moses also told the Israelites that God expected them to walk in his ways.

This life offers us two paths. One is the path of the world. This is the path that is opposed to God. It does not bow to his authority and does not follow his will.

The other path is, of course, the exact opposite. It is the path of God that both accepts God's authority and practises his will.

God's path is the one that brings blessing into our lives, as the author of Psalm 1 points out:

> Blessed is the man
> Who walks not in the counsel of the ungodly,
> Nor stands in the path of sinners,
> Nor sits in the seat of the scornful;
> But his delight is in the law of the LORD,
> And in His law he meditates day and night.
>
> (vv. 1–2)

We are to love him (v. 12)

Moses also affirms that God expects his people to love him.

God does not want us to meet his expectations out of a bare

sense of duty. He does not want a sighing, reluctant compliance from us. He rather wants us to live up to his expectations out of hearts that are thrilled to do so.

Why should we not love God? He has blessed his people with many good things and with the supremely good thing—salvation from eternal destruction through the redeeming work of his Son. How can we not love such a God? Let us, then, join Isaac Watts in singing,

> Love so amazing, so divine,
> Demands my soul, my life, my all.[2]

How sad it is that many of us are in the same condition as the church of Ephesus—the condition of lesser love (Rev. 2:4). We don't love the Lord as we once did! How we need revival!

We are to serve him wholeheartedly (v. 12)

This means that we are to devote ourselves to living for his honour and advancing his kingdom. And we are to do these things, not reluctantly and begrudgingly, but sincerely and fervently. We should each aspire to say with the apostle Paul that we serve God with our spirit (Rom. 1:9).

How much of our service today is of the shuffling, half-hearted variety! True revival will take this away from us and replace it with an eagerness that will cause each of us continually to ask, 'What can I do for the Lord?'

We are to keep his commandments (v. 13)

This is the last in Moses' list of God's expectations for his people. It is somewhat similar to walking in God's ways, but now the matter is made even more explicit and clear.

God expects his people to obey him—fully and gladly! What he tells us to do, we are to do, and what he tells us not to do, we are to refrain from doing. As Moses makes clear, the commandments of God are for our good (v. 13).

The devil would have us believe otherwise. He insists that the commandments of God are designed to take the joy out of living. But the devil always has been and is a liar. It is sin that wrecks and ruins. The commandments of God ensure our well-being.

Matthew Henry summarizes it thus: 'Having given up ourselves to his service, we must make his revealed will our rule in everything, perform all he prescribes, forbear all he forbids, firmly believing that all the statutes he commands us are for our good.'[3]

Just as we have standards for various aspects of our lives, so God has a standard for the lives of his people. While we readily accept standards in other areas of life, we rebel at the thought of God having a standard for our lives. But he does. We find those standards in the Bible. Let's make it our daily business to study it and practise it.

Reflect on these points

1. *The angels of heaven stand in awe of God. How much more, then, should we!*

2. *This life offers us two paths: the path of the world and*

the path of God. God's path is the one that brings blessing into our lives.

3. *God does not want us to meet his expectations out of a bare sense of duty but out of hearts that are thrilled to do so.*

4. *The devil would have us believe that the commandments of God are designed to take the joy out of living. But the devil always has been and is a liar. The commandments of God ensure our well-being.*

God's people have every reason to live up to his expectations

For this reason we also, since the day we heard it, do not cease to pray for you ...

That you may walk worthy of the Lord, fully pleasing Him ...

Giving thanks to the Father who has qualified us to be partakers of the inheritance of the saints in the light.

He has delivered us from the power of darkness and conveyed us into the kingdom of the Son of His love,

In whom we have redemption through His blood, the forgiveness of sins.

Colossians 1:9–14

We have established two things: God has a people, and he has certain expectations for his people. But what about these people? Do they have any reason to live up to God's expectations? Or does God ask too much of them?

Our text is one of several passages of Scripture that powerfully answer these questions. The apostle Paul is calling his readers to live in a worthy and pleasing manner (v. 10). We might say that he is telling them to live up to God's expectations.

One of the components for living in a worthy and pleasing manner is 'giving thanks to the Father'. Charles Erdman is surely right to observe, 'The very designation of God by the name "Father" might well awaken a spirit of gratitude. It points to the loving Source from which comes "every good and perfect gift".'[1]

Paul's emphasis on thanksgiving speaks pointedly about our general demeanour, the way in which we 'carry' ourselves. We all have our difficulties and our burdens, but we should never allow these things to obscure our blessings. How blessed we are! Let us, then, go along life's way with our hearts rejoicing and with our mouths filled with thanksgiving. Sour Christians are not walking in a worthy manner and are not pleasing to the Lord.

The major thing for which Christians are to be thankful is, of course, their salvation. The joy for facing life's hardships can only come from hearts that have been diligently schooled in redemption's work. It cannot be stressed too strongly that Paul addresses thanksgiving for the Colossians' salvation exclusively to God. Not a shred of credit is given to the Colossians themselves. The reason is because salvation is entirely of God. Jean Daillé said of salvation, 'This wholly appertaineth unto God.'[2] John Newton celebrated the same truth with these words:

> 'Twas grace that taught my heart to fear,
> And grace my fears relieved.
> How precious did that grace appear
> The hour I first believed![3]

Paul could have told the Colossians to be thankful for their salvation and left it at that. But he always found it quite difficult to merely mention salvation. Once he rubbed up against the topic, he invariably found himself glorying in it. He does so here by using five exhilarating phrases. There is no larger or more common failing these days than the failure to truly glory in salvation. Carefully pondering Paul's phrases will go a long way toward keeping us from this failure.

Qualified (v. 12)

First, he says the Father 'has qualified us to be partakers of the inheritance of the saints in the light'. R. C. H. Lenski happily translates 'qualified us' as 'sufficiented us'.[4]

The inheritance of the saints in the light begins in this life and culminates in heaven. The apostle is telling us that God first fits us to share the lot or portion of the saints in this life. This portion is 'in the light'. Believers, like everyone else, came into this world in a state of spiritual darkness, but God in grace has called them out of that darkness 'into His marvelous light' (1 Peter 2:9).

Paul is repeating to the Colossians that which he affirmed to the Ephesians: 'For you were once darkness, but now you are light in the Lord. Walk as children of light' (Eph. 5:8).

The children of light will finally enter the kingdom of light described by the apostle John in these words:

> The city had no need of the sun or of the moon to shine in it, for the glory of God illuminated it. The Lamb is its light. And the nations of those who are saved shall walk in its light, and the kings of the earth bring their glory and honor into it. Its gates shall not be shut at all by day (there shall be no night there).
>
> (Rev. 21:23–25)

The children of light will enter there only because they have been qualified by the Lord. We are sinners by nature. We have the darkness of sin in us and with us and, therefore, cannot enjoy the light that God has prepared in eternity. In order to be partakers of God's inheritance in light we have to be perfectly righteous, but we have no righteousness. Furthermore, there is absolutely nothing we can do to provide it. But—wonderful news!—God himself qualifies sinners to be partakers of the light of glory. In his Son, Jesus Christ, God provided the righteousness that he demands of us and he applies that righteousness to each believer.

We could not be qualified for heaven without it, but with it we can take as our own the words of Count von Zinzendorf:

> Jesus, Thy blood and righteousness
> My beauty are, my glorious dress;
> 'Midst flaming worlds, in these arrayed,
> With joy shall I lift up my head.
>
> Bold shall I stand in Thy great day;
> For who aught to my charge shall lay?
> Fully through Thee absolved I am
> From sin and fear, from guilt and shame.

Delivered (v. 13)

In the second place, thanksgiving is due to God because 'He has delivered us from the power of darkness ...'

We all come into this world as part of Satan's kingdom. Oh, the darkness of this kingdom! It is the darkness of ignorance.

The citizens of this kingdom have their minds blinded so they cannot see their true condition (2 Cor. 4:3–4). It is the darkness of death. Those who stay in this kingdom will eventually be enveloped by eternal death (2 Peter 2:17; Jude 12–13).

Believers are to rejoice because they have been taken out of this kingdom by the Lord Jesus Christ. Through his redeeming death on the cross, he decisively defeated Satan and delivered all believers from his kingdom of darkness.

While the apostle has not yet mentioned the 'basic principles of the world' (Col. 2:8, 20), he has already shown the folly of devotion to these spiritual beings. Christ has qualified his people for heaven, and no one, including these spirit-beings, can disqualify them. Christ has delivered his people from the domain of darkness, and no one can reclaim them.

Conveyed (v. 13)

The third of Paul's glorious phrases is '... and conveyed us into the kingdom of the Son of His love ...' This phrase refers to the practice of removing people from one country and settling them as colonists in another. How big is salvation? It amounts to nothing less than a change of kingdom. It takes us out of Satan's kingdom and resettles us as citizens of God's kingdom. It would have been unspeakably glorious just for God to do the former. How astonishing that he would go so far as to do the latter!

The new kingdom in which believers are settled is 'the kingdom of the Son of His love'. This tells us how very certain believers can be of their new citizenship. God loves his Son

31

with an immeasurable and indestructible love. Those who are in Christ can rest assured that this same love is extended to them.

Because of this transfer from one kingdom to another, each believer can say a hearty 'Amen!' to the words of Paul to the Philippians: 'For our citizenship is in heaven, from which we also eagerly wait for the Savior, the Lord Jesus Christ, who will transform our lowly body that it may be conformed to His glorious body, according to the working by which He is able even to subdue all things to Himself' (Phil. 3:20–21).

Redeemed (v. 14)

Paul's fourth phrase is: '… in whom we have redemption through His blood …' The word 'redeemed' means 'to buy back'. Although believers belonged to God by virtue of creation, they were all taken prisoner by sin and held by the chain of God's law. That law demands that the sinner be punished with eternal separation from God.

Believers, however, have been redeemed by the blood of Christ, that is, by the death of Christ. On the cross, Jesus received the eternal separation his people deserve. The law of God was, therefore, satisfied, and they were freed. God paid the ransom for them through the death of his Son.

Forgiven (v. 14)

The last of Paul's glorious phrases is 'the forgiveness of sins'. The word 'forgive' means 'to send away' or 'to cancel a debt'. Satan would have us believe that our sins constitute an insurmountable barrier to entering heaven. He points to those sins and says, 'Look at them! You are not fit to enter heaven!'

But we do not fear a creditor pointing to a statement if that statement has stamped on it these words: PAID IN FULL. And Christians need not fear Satan pointing to their sin debt because Jesus paid it in full.

Qualified! Delivered! Conveyed! Redeemed! Forgiven! If we do not feel joyful astonishment over salvation, it must in large measure be due to failing to ponder what these words convey about what we were in sin and what we are in Christ.

Reflect on these points

1. *We all have difficulties and burdens, but we should never allow these things to obscure our blessings. How blessed we are! Sour Christians are not walking in a worthy manner and are not pleasing to the Lord.*

2. *The joy for facing life's hardships can only come from hearts that have been diligently schooled in redemption's work.*

3. *Christ has qualified his people for heaven, and no one can disqualify them. Christ has delivered his people from the domain of darkness, and no one can reclaim them.*

4. *We do not fear a creditor pointing to a statement if that statement has stamped on it these words: PAID IN FULL. And Christians need not fear Satan pointing to their sin debt because Jesus paid it in full.*

God's people sometimes backslide

Thus says the LORD *of hosts, the God of Israel: 'Add your burnt offerings to your sacrifices and eat meat.*

'For I did not speak to your fathers, or command them in the day that I brought them out of the land of Egypt, concerning burnt offerings or sacrifices.

'But this is what I commanded them, saying, "Obey My voice, and I will be your God, and you shall be My people. And walk in all the ways that I have commanded you, that it may be well with you."

'Yet they did not obey or incline their ear, but followed the counsels and the dictates of their evil hearts, and went backward and not forward.

'Since the day that your fathers came out of the land of Egypt until this day, I have even sent to you all My servants the prophets, daily rising up early and sending them.

'Yet they did not obey Me or incline their ear, but stiffened their neck. They did worse than their fathers.'

Jeremiah 7:21–26

We come now to an ugly truth: God's people are weak and imperfect. This means we often fail to live up to God's expectations, even though the reasons to live for God are plentiful. King Solomon was right to ask, 'Who can say, "I have made my heart clean, I am pure from my sin"?' (Prov. 20:9). The apostle John got it right when he wrote, 'If we say that we have no sin, we deceive ourselves, and the truth is not in us' (1 John 1:8).

We can see this truth written large in the lives of the

men and women of the Bible. Noah, Lot, Jacob, Samson, Naomi, David, Solomon, Jonah, Simon Peter—all speak very pointedly to us about the ever-present danger of slipping into sin and slipping away from God.

The nations of Israel and Judah do the same. At one point, God said of Israel, 'My people are bent on backsliding from Me. Though they call to the Most High, none at all exalt Him' (Hosea 11:7). In Jeremiah 7, we find the Lord issuing this devastating indictment on the nation of Judah: '... this is what I commanded them ... Yet they did not obey or incline their ear, but followed the counsels and the dictates of their evil hearts, and went backward and not forward' (vv. 23–24).

We are face to face, then, with this reality: God's people have a tendency to backslide. This reality is so commonplace and so damaging that we must take some time to raise and answer some questions about it.

What is backsliding?

The word itself tells us all we need to know. To 'backslide' is to slide back from a level or point previously attained.

To be converted to Christ means to be changed (2 Cor. 5:17). Conversion changes our thinking. We see ourselves as guilty sinners before a holy God and facing eternal destruction. But, thank God, we also understand that there is forgiveness for our sins and right standing with God through Jesus Christ. When we are converted, the gospel is exceedingly precious to us.

Conversion also changes our desires. It gives us an

enjoyment of the things of God, a zeal for him, a desire and determination to do his work. It gives us a love for his people.

Conversion also changes our doing. We begin to order our lives in keeping with his commandments.

To 'backslide' is to step back or to slip away from these things. When we backslide, we turn away from God with our minds. The truth of God is not as precious to us as it once was. We turn away from God in our desires. Our hearts are no longer in our service of God as they once were. There is now a coldness of heart instead of a warmth. And we also turn away from God in our behaviour. We begin to neglect the things we ought to do and to do the things we ought not to do.

Proverbs 14:14 tells us that the backslider is 'filled with his own ways'. Richard Owen Roberts writes, 'There you have it—a backslider is a person who was once emptied of his own ways and filled with the ways of God, but gradually allowed his own ways to seep back in until he was all but empty of God and full of himself again.'[1]

Let me hasten to add that backsliding does not mean the loss of salvation. No child of God can lose his or her salvation. Scripture makes that abundantly plain (John 10:28–29; 1 Peter 1:5). Salvation is God's good work, and he will never abandon it (Phil. 1:6). The Lord Jesus is both the author and the finisher of faith (Heb. 12:2). If faith was ours, we could well worry about losing it, but faith is God's. He is the giver of it, and he will sustain it.

A backslider, then, is like a man on a ship. He can fall on the deck, but he will never fall overboard.

But a child of God can sink terribly low! And part of the misery of backsliding is that it causes the believer to doubt his or her salvation.

That brings us to a second question:

Why does God allow his people to backslide?

We surely agree that God could prevent his people from backsliding. Why does he not do so?

We will not have the complete answer to this question until we finally come into his presence. The ways of God are ever mysterious. They are, as Paul says, 'past finding out' (Rom. 11:33).

We can only say that, by allowing us to backslide, God shows us how very weak we are, how very strong Satan is, and how desperately we need God.

Parents know something about this. Wise parents do not protect their children from every single thing that comes along. Sometimes, they allow their children to make bad choices and experience the results of those bad choices so that they will learn not to make even worse choices in the future. God is always wiser than the wisest parent.

We have to understand what God is doing in our lives. Many have the wrong job description for God. They think it is God's job to make life comfortable, pleasant and convenient. When something comes along that makes them uncomfortable or causes them to be inconvenienced, they are ready to pronounce God as a failure.

But God has never told us that he is after our comfort and convenience! He has rather told us that it is his purpose to conform us to the image of his Son (Rom. 8:29). He wants to grow us to spiritual maturity. Doesn't it make sense to say, then, that this purpose will require God to go about things differently from how he would if his purpose were simply to make life easy for us?

All will become clear when we come into his presence; then our testimony will be that God has done all things well. We will even bless him for letting us get burned by our backsliding because we will recognize that the burning was part and parcel of the maturing process.

Let's turn our attention to yet another question about backsliding:

What causes backsliding?

So God allows his people to backslide. He does not cause it, but chooses for his own wise purposes to allow it. What, then, are some of the causes? Here are a few of the main reasons why we backslide:

- Discouragement. We have tried to serve the Lord and have seen little success. So we feel justified in easing up.
- Love of ease and comfort.
- Carelessness about the means of grace. God has appointed certain things that promote spiritual growth

and vitality, such as the preaching and teaching of God's Word, prayer, Bible study and the Lord's Supper. But if we do not use them, or do not use them in the right way, we do not reap benefits from them.

- Not being mindful of the greatness of our salvation, which is ever the antidote to backsliding! We must, therefore, always remind ourselves of our 'so great ... salvation' (Heb. 2:3).
- Not being mindful of the costliness of backsliding. Its terrible results include damaging our testimony before unbelievers and impairing our comforts as believers.
- Disappointment with God or with another Christian.

If we had to leave it at this point, we would feel nothing but gloom. But, thank God, we can answer yet another question:

What is the cure for backsliding?

No one has answered this question better than the prophet Hosea: 'Take words with you, and return to the LORD. Say to Him, "Take away all iniquity; receive us graciously ..."' (Hosea 14:2). And Hosea assures us that the Lord will respond in this way: 'I will heal their backsliding, I will love them freely ...' (14:4).

Reflect on these points

1. Backsliding does not mean the loss of salvation. No child of God can lose his or her salvation. Scripture makes that abundantly plain.

2. *By allowing us to backslide, God shows us how very weak we are, how very strong Satan is, and how desperately we need God.*

3. *God has never told us that he is after our comfort and convenience! He has rather told us that it is his purpose to conform us to the image of his Son.*

4. *When we come into God's presence, we will bless him for letting us get burned by our backsliding because we will recognize that the burning was part and parcel of the maturing process.*

God revives
his people

Moses took his tent and pitched it outside the camp, far from the camp, and called it the tabernacle of meeting. And it came to pass that everyone who sought the LORD *went out to the tabernacle of meeting which was outside the camp ...*

And it came to pass, when Moses entered the tabernacle, that the pillar of cloud descended and stood at the door of the tabernacle, and the LORD *talked with Moses.*

Exodus 33:7, 9

Then Samuel spoke to all the house of Israel, saying, 'If you return to the LORD *with all your hearts, then put away the foreign gods and the Ashtoreths from among you, and prepare your hearts for the* LORD, *and serve Him only; and He will deliver you from the hand of the Philistines.'*

So the children of Israel put away the Baals and the Ashtoreths, and served the LORD *only.*

1 Samuel 7:3-4

We have now put four things in place: God has a people, God has certain expectations of his people, God's people have every reason to live up to his expectations, and God's people often fail to live up to his expectations.

If we had to leave it there, we would be enveloped with gloom. But, happily, we can go on to add another truth: God has been known to revive his people when they have fallen into a pattern of failure.

We have no trouble finding this truth in the Bible. There are plenty of examples of God reviving individual saints:

Abraham, Jacob, David, Elijah, Jonah and Simon Peter. There are also examples of God supplying corporate revival. Richard Owen Roberts includes the following in a list of such revivals in the Old Testament:

- under Moses (Exod. chs. 32ff.).
- under Samuel (1 Sam. 7)
- under David (2 Sam. 6–7)
- under Hezekiah (2 Chr. 29–32)
- under Zerubbabel (Ezra 1–6)
- under Joel (Joel 2:12–27).[1]

In his book *Revival! A People Saturated with God*, Brian H. Edwards lists fifty-seven revivals from 1150 to 1973.[2] Jonathan Edwards declared,

> … it may be observed that from the fall of man to our day, the work of redemption in its effect has mainly been carried on by remarkable outpourings of the Spirit of God. Though there be a more constant influence of God's Spirit always in some degree attending his ordinances, yet the way in which the greatest things have been done in carrying on this work always has been remarkable pourings out of the Spirit at special seasons of mercy.[3]

In this chapter, we will look at two of the Old Testament revivals mentioned above. We do so merely to remind ourselves that we are not on a fool's errand when we seek revival. God does revive his people! We will look at the revivals that took place in Israel under Moses and Samuel so we can be reminded that there is always hope for revival; that God's people, no matter how far they have strayed and how grievously they have sinned, are not beyond the reach of God's reviving grace.

The revival under Moses (Exod. 33:7–11)

The centrepiece of this revival was the tent of meeting that Moses erected outside the camp of Israel. We must not confuse this tent with the tabernacle, which had not yet been constructed (Exod. 35–40).

This tent of meeting was Moses' response to a shocking lapse of the people into idolatry. While he had been receiving the Law of God on Mount Sinai, the people had worshipped a golden calf (32:1–5)!

Although Moses had dealt very sternly with the idolatry (32:19–29), its cloud was still hanging heavy over Israel. The Lord was so grieved over the sin of the people that he told Moses that he, the Lord, would not go to the promised land in their midst but would only send his Angel before them (33:1–3). These words were 'bad news' (33:4).

Moses set up the tent of meeting for the purpose of seeking the presence of the Lord. He knew that it was not enough for the people to turn away from their idols; they must also wholeheartedly turn back to God.

This tells us that God's people can expect revival when they so feel the burden of the times that they are willing to take special measures to seek God's face.

There was an encouraging sign along these lines even

before Moses set up the tent. Exodus 33:4 says, 'And when the people heard this bad news, they mourned, and no one put on his ornaments.' These people, realizing the gravity of their situation, were unwilling to go about their lives as usual. They felt such inward grief over the loss of God's presence that they expressed it outwardly.

In doing so, they put themselves far ahead of today's church. How few grieve over the loss of God's presence! As long as the church machinery grinds on—churning out more and more programmes and producing good numbers—church leaders are willing to overlook the absence of any real spiritual power. And as long as their lives are comfortable, individual Christians are willing to do the same.

A 'business as usual' attitude will never bring revival. Many of the people of Israel understood this. Do we? Martyn Lloyd-Jones wrote, '… generally the very first thing that happens, and which eventually leads to a great revival, is that one man, or a group of men, suddenly begin to feel this burden, and they feel the burden so much that they are led to do something about it.'[4] Erroll Hulse observes, 'When the Holy Spirit moves to create a deep desire for revival in the churches and awakening in society he does that from within, by stirring up a burden in the hearts of his people and prompting them to prayer.'[5]

Moses' tent of meeting achieved its purpose. This passage tells us that the pillar of cloud, which symbolized God's presence, 'stood at the door of the tabernacle' (v. 9).

That cloud had been withdrawn while the people were

occupied with their calf. But now, as a result of Moses and many of the people seeking God, it came back. And the Lord said to Moses, 'My Presence will go with you, and I will give you rest' (v. 14).

Moses' tent of meeting brings us to this encouraging conclusion: If we will seek the Lord, we can rest assured that he will be found. We can be confident of this because of the promise he has given: '… if My people who are called by My name will humble themselves, and pray and seek My face, and turn from their wicked ways, then I will hear from heaven, and will forgive their sin and heal their land' (2 Chr. 7:14).

The revival under Samuel (1 Sam. 7:2–14)

We now hit the Fast Forward button on the history of the nation of Israel to arrive at the time of Samuel. Israel had now been in the land of Canaan for many years. (God had indeed gone with them and blessed them!) But it was a dark and brooding time—all because the people had been playing fast and loose with the commandments of God! People and priests were equally guilty.

To bring his people to their senses, God raised up the Philistines to oppress them. The oppression reached its height, or depth, when the Israelites carried the ark of God into battle and the Philistines made off with it (1 Sam. 4:1–11)! The ark should never have been there. It was to be kept in the Most Holy Place of the tabernacle, but Hophni and Phinehas, two vile specimens and sorry excuses for priests, were so spiritually obtuse that they thought they could gain victory by carrying the ark to the battlefield. Although they spent most of their time thumbing their noses at God, they thought they could still secure his presence by toting around his ark!

The Philistines soon learned that they could not live with the ark, and, through a series of fascinating events, it was returned to Israel (1 Sam. 5:1–6:16). But true religious vitality did not accompany it. For twenty long years, the ark sat in the house of Abinadab (1 Sam. 7:1), and Israel languished in spiritual apathy.

Suddenly, a bright ray of hope pierced the gloom: 'And all the house of Israel lamented after the LORD' (1 Sam. 7:2).

How are we to explain this lamenting? The next phrase gives us the answer: 'Then Samuel spoke to all the house of Israel ...' (v. 3).

We may be sure that Samuel was quietly and doggedly working to spread the Word of God throughout Israel during the twenty years of spiritual declension. Now that quiet ministry began to bear fruit. Gordon Keddie writes, '... trouble concentrated their minds and, bit by bit, they came to see that God was their only hope. The ministry of Samuel during these years would have had its leavening effect in bringing this national spiritual crisis to the boil.'[6]

The people of Israel finally came to see their desperate condition. They recognized at long last that their problems were all due to the fact that they had driven the Lord away because of their sins, and they began to yearn for him again. It should go without saying that it is impossible to yearn for God without yearning for his Word. This is where Samuel came in.

PUTTING AWAY

Samuel emphasized that there could be no true revival as long as the people continued to hold on to idols. The Ashtoreths mentioned in this passage (v. 3) were particularly lewd representations of Canaanite goddesses.

The people demonstrated their seriousness and sincerity about revival by doing as Samuel demanded (v. 4).

COMING TOGETHER

The work of revival in verses 1 through 4 was probably done on a village-by-village level as Samuel travelled the length and breadth of the nation. But when the work progressed to a certain point, Samuel realized that it was time to call the whole nation together for a solemn assembly (vv. 5–6). This he did at Mizpah.

POURING OUT

When the people came together for the assembly, Samuel drew water and 'poured it out before the LORD' (v. 6). This was a visible and open display of what was going on in their hearts; Samuel was picturing the pouring out of their hearts in true repentance before God.

Another indication of their repentance was fasting (v. 6). Food lost its appeal to them because they were lost in the larger concern of getting right with God.

The pouring out of their hearts before God in true

repentance led to a pouring out of public confession as the people cried out, 'We have sinned against the LORD' (v. 6).

The experience of Israel under Samuel provides an agenda for all who long to see God revive his people. We must admit that revival is always the prerogative of a sovereign God. We cannot wire it or produce it. But we can and should give ourselves to coming together with other believers to seek the Lord, to put away our idols and to pour out our hearts in true repentance. Serious and devoted attention to these matters will in and of itself be evidence that the sovereign God has already been pleased to begin his work of revival within us.

As we noted at the outset, several revivals occurred during the Old Testament era, but the revivals under Moses and Samuel tell us all that we need to know. God does revive his people! Let us, then, heed the words of Samuel: 'If you return to the LORD with all your hearts, then put away the foreign gods … from among you, and prepare your hearts for the LORD, and serve Him only …' (1 Sam. 7:3).

Reflect on these points

1. *God's people can expect revival when they so feel the burden of the times that they are willing to take special measures to seek God's face.*

2. *How few grieve over the loss of God's presence! As long as the church machinery grinds on, church leaders are willing to overlook the absence of any real spiritual power. And as long as their lives are comfortable, individual Christians are willing to do the same.*

3. *It is impossible to yearn for God without yearning for his Word.*

4. *We should give ourselves to coming together with other believers to seek the Lord, to put away our idols and to pour out our hearts in true repentance.*

Revival glory

God makes himself known

And it came to pass, at the time of the offering of the evening sacrifice, that Elijah the prophet came near and said, 'Lord God of Abraham, Isaac, and Israel, let it be known this day that You are God in Israel and I am Your servant, and that I have done all these things at Your word.

'Hear me, O Lord, hear me, that this people may know that You are the Lord God, and that You have turned their hearts back to You again.'

Then the fire of the Lord fell and consumed the burnt sacrifice, and the wood and the stones and the dust, and it licked up the water that was in the trench.

Now when all the people saw it, they fell on their faces; and they said, 'The Lord, He is God! The Lord, He is God!'

1 Kings 18:36–39

All true religion flows from knowing that God exists, knowing what he is like and knowing that he is near.

Odd as it sounds, it is nevertheless true that it is possible for God's people to begin living as if God does not exist, or as if he is very far away. They can live as if the God in whom they believe is quite different from the God of the Bible.

When God's people fall into such a low and lamentable state, they urgently need God to visit them in such a way that they are fully persuaded that he is there and they know exactly what he is like. They need him to visit them in such a way that they are able to say with Daniel, 'But there is a God in heaven' (Dan. 2:28).

Revival is nothing less than God visiting his people in

a special and powerful way. It is God sweeping away the cobwebs of doubt. It is God removing any notion that he is distant and making it known that he is near.

The people of Israel had not quite forgotten all about God. They still professed to believe in him, and they still continued to go through the motions of worshipping him. But God and his ways seemed old to them.

Baal, on the other hand, was new and exciting. His religion stirred their feelings, blending religious duties with gratification of fleshly desires. Baal was the weather god. He supposedly brought rain for the crops, and his devotees could persuade him to provide rain by practising sexual rites.

Elijah, the prophet of God, seemed tame and dull. He was the representative of old religion, the religion of the fathers. He was the representative of the religion that simply said: Believe God's Word and obey his commandments.

The nation was now met on Mount Carmel to test a proposition. Could they have it both ways? Could they serve both God and Baal? Elijah framed the issue in such a way that no thinking person could argue for a synthesis of mutually exclusive options. Israel had been hobbling along in an impossible contradiction (1 Kings 18:21). The issue needed to be decided. God or Baal: which was it to be?

Elijah proposed a contest of fire. He and the 450 prophets of Baal would prepare sacrifices, and the god who sent fire to consume his sacrifice would be acknowledged as God (vv. 23–24).

The failure of Baal

The prophets of Baal were licking their chops! Elijah had played right into their hands! Fire was no problem for their god. He was the storm-god who caused the thunder to roll and the lightning to flash. They would make short work of Elijah and his God! So they began to pray, 'O Baal, hear us!' (v. 26). But hour after hour passed, and there was no lightning. These men worked themselves up into an emotional frenzy, jumping on the altar and crying out, but it was to no avail. Cutting themselves with their lances, as if to draw the sympathy of their god, did not work either.

Their allotted time ended in pathetic failure. The 450 prophets were left hoarse from their crying and covered with their own blood, but their sacrifice stood unconsumed. There was 'no voice; no one answered' (v. 26). There was no answer because there was no god. Baal was a figment of the imagination and a creation of those who wanted a religion to pander to their fleshly desires.

The fire of God

Elijah had stood by in amazed bemusement as the prophets of Baal went through their gyrations. He knew theirs was a hopeless task. He could ridicule them and their god (v. 27) because he had nothing to fear. Baal existed only in human minds.

Now Baal was discredited and it was his turn. He went about his task in workmanlike fashion. There was an old altar to the Lord there, long since broken down: a mute and powerful testimony to the fact that Israel had long since forsaken the faith of the fathers. It took twelve stones to repair that altar: a pointed reminder that the twelve tribes of Israel were to be united in faith in the living God.

With the altar repaired, Elijah had twelve pots of water poured on his sacrifice. Where was water to be found in a parched land that had suffered three-plus years of drought? From the nearby Mediterranean Sea!

The sacrifice was drenched and water stood in the trench that Elijah had dug around the sacrifice. He would now ask God to do the seemingly impossible—send fire from heaven to consume a wet sacrifice.

There was a solemn air about Elijah. He didn't tell a few jokes to 'loosen up' the crowd and get them on his side. The issue was far too serious for clowning and joking. He didn't try to 'out-emotion' the prophets of Baal. He humbly prayed that God would make himself known as God ('let it be known this day that You are God in Israel', v. 36; 'that this people may know that You are the Lord God', v. 37).

This was no prolonged ordeal, as when the prophets of Baal had their turn. There was no jumping, no cutting and no waiting. Elijah prayed, and 'the fire of the Lord fell and consumed the burnt sacrifice' (v. 38).

The people of Israel responded by falling on their faces and crying, 'The Lord, He is God! The Lord, He is God!' (v. 39).

The God of the fire

God made himself known that day. He also showed himself to be a certain kind of God:

- the awesome God, who is worthy of reverence, worship and service
- the jealous God, who would not tolerate Baal or any other rival
- the faithful God, who will not 'write off' his people even when they go into sin
- the gracious God, who revealed himself to his people although they were unworthy and undeserving
- the powerful God, who can easily do that which seems impossible
- the just and holy God, who judges those who reject him (the prophets of Baal were slain that day—v. 40).

Are we conscious of these things—not in a theoretical or academic way, but in a real and powerful way? If we are conscious that God is awesome, we will be showing reverence. If we are aware that he is jealous, we will not be putting other things ahead of him. If we realize his faithfulness and graciousness, we will be grateful to him. If we know he is powerful, we will be earnestly seeking manifestations of his power. If we are aware that he judges, we will not be so casual and careless about spiritual things. We will not trifle with him or his commandments.

In normal times, people speculate about God and discuss what he is like. In times of revival, there is no need to discuss whether he exists and what he is like. Revival makes it all perfectly plain, and the discussion ends.

We definitely need the fire of God today, but not to consume a physical sacrifice. We need fire that will consume false doctrine, burn out the sin in our lives, destroy our idols and eliminate our dependence on the flesh. But we must not let the fire of God crowd out the God of the fire. Our most pressing need is to know God himself. Perhaps the reason why we do not see spectacular manifestations as Israel did on Mount Carmel is because we always have a tendency to focus on the manifestations rather than on God. Our sinful nature ever makes us more concerned with the gifts than with the Giver.

Let us never forget another occasion when the fire of God fell. When Jesus was hanging on the cross, he experienced not a physical fire, but rather the fire of God's wrath. By enduring that wrath in the stead of sinners, he made it possible for all who believe to know the God of the fire.

Reflect on these points

1. *It is possible for God's people to live as if God does not exist, or as if he is very far away. Then they urgently need God to visit them in such a way that they are fully persuaded that he is there and they know exactly what he is like.*

2. *Are we conscious that God is awesome? That he is jealous? That he is faithful and gracious? That he is powerful? That he judges?*

3. *We need the fire of God today—fire that will consume false doctrine, burn out the sin in our lives, destroy our idols and eliminate our dependence on the flesh. But our most pressing need is to know God himself.*

God's people
are humbled

In the year that King Uzziah died, I saw the Lord sitting on a throne, high and lifted up, and the train of His robe filled the temple.

Above it stood seraphim; each one had six wings: with two he covered his face, with two he covered his feet, and with two he flew.

And one cried to another and said: 'Holy, holy, holy is the LORD of hosts; The whole earth is full of His glory!'

And the posts of the door were shaken by the voice of him who cried out, and the house was filled with smoke.

So I said: 'Woe is me, for I am undone! Because I am a man of unclean lips, And I dwell in the midst of a people of unclean lips; For my eyes have seen the King, The LORD of hosts.'

Then one of the seraphim flew to me, having in his hand a live coal which he had taken with the tongs from the altar.

And he touched my mouth with it, and said: 'Behold, this has touched your lips; Your iniquity is taken away, And your sin purged.'

Isaiah 6:1–7

There is an undeniable link between revival and humility. When the recovered Book of the Law was read to King Josiah, he humbled himself before God, tore his clothes and wept (2 Chr. 34:27).

The Lord himself connected revival with humility in these words: 'I dwell in the high and holy place, with him who has a contrite and humble spirit, to revive the spirit of the humble, and to revive the heart of the contrite ones' (Isa. 57:15).

Revival exalts God, and God cannot be lifted high until we are laid low. If God is on the throne, we must be in the dust. The best-loved of all revival texts says, '... if My people who are called by My name will humble themselves ... then I will hear from heaven, and will forgive their sin and heal their land' (2 Chr. 7:14).

Humility is to be the hallmark of Christians. After all, we became Christians by being brought low. Christians know the reality and depth of their sin and their complete inability to save themselves. Christians know that they are utterly shut up to the grace of God.

However, while we enter God's family through the door of humility, we can, after entering, be filled with pride. No child of God is immune. Uzziah and Hezekiah were godly kings but the heart of each was 'lifted up' (2 Chr. 26:16; 32:25).

To ask how near we are to revival is to ask how near we are to humility. We often seem to be very far from it. Church leaders, who should be in the forefront of seeking revival, are frequently filled with pride, using worship services to call attention to themselves and to present themselves as clever, charming and witty. God will not share the stage with another! If we occupy it, he will depart.

There is no greater expression of pride than pastors laying aside the clear teachings of the Word of God on God's holiness, human sin, divine judgement, repentance and the atoning work of Christ, to present messages that are more palatable to their hearers. How often we think we know better than God! This is raw, undiluted pride!

Pride stems from poor spiritual eyesight. Revival corrects our vision. It enables us to see the truth about God and about ourselves, and the sight of each will drive pride from us.

The prophet Isaiah can be of help to us on this matter of restored sight. By means of a vision, he saw both God and himself. He was born in Jerusalem around 760 BC. He prophesied in the kingdom of Judah during the reigns of Jotham, Ahaz and Hezekiah. It is thought by many that he lived into the evil reign of the wicked Manasseh and that he was executed by being 'sawn in two' (Heb. 11:37).

The years of Isaiah's life and ministry were tumultuous and threatening. Assyria was the major world power at the time, and Judah's sister kingdom, Israel, fell to her during Isaiah's ministry. Judah herself came perilously close to doing the same during the reign of Hezekiah, but was miraculously spared (Isa. 36:1–37:38).

But the real threat to the people of Judah was not the Assyrians but their own lack of faithful obedience to their God. The prophecy of Isaiah wasted no time in getting to this. The opening chapters tell of a nation that was maintaining the outward show of religion while ignoring its demands in daily life. Because of that, the people of Judah were firmly in the clutches of a crass materialism that caused them to oppress the poor and to disregard justice. Life in Judah in Isaiah's time was proof that when men are not in a right relationship to God, they can't be in a right relationship with each other.

Isaiah 6 makes it clear that Isaiah was God's man for this terrible time. He had been serving as a prophet before the experience recorded in this chapter; what we have here could be viewed as his recommissioning. We can well understand his need for that kind of thing; the lack of receptivity to his message must have made him wonder if he had been truly called of God. His experience in the temple forever settled that issue.

Isaiah saw the Lord (vv. 1–4)

The good king Uzziah had died after a glorious reign of fifty years. The impression we get is that Isaiah went to the temple with the death of Uzziah on his mind. Evidently, this was to Isaiah a calamity of the first order, and he was undoubtedly deeply perplexed and uncertain about the future of the nation. He may very well have viewed Uzziah as a bulwark against disaster for the nation. What would happen with Uzziah gone?

But there was no need to fear. There in the temple, Isaiah saw the Lord 'sitting on a throne, high and lifted up'.

THE THRONE AND THE ROBE (V. 1)

The throne indicates sovereign authority, and the fact that the Lord was sitting there implies that he was not in a panic but was completely at peace. Isaiah may have been upset, but the Lord was not moved by circumstances or calamity.

Isaiah also noted that the Lord's robe filled the temple. This suggests that there is no limit to God's sovereignty. It extends to every nook and cranny of all reality.

THE SERAPHIM (VV. 2–3)

Seraphim surrounded the throne of God. The word 'seraphim' means 'burning ones'. This may mean that the appearance of these beings was such that it looked as if they were on fire.

Each of these heavenly creatures had six wings. With two they covered their faces, to express their reverence for God. With two more wings they covered their feet (the reference is probably to all their lower extremities), to conceal as much of themselves as possible. By doing so, they expressed their complete sense of unworthiness in the presence of their glorious God. Albert Barnes rightly concludes, '… if the pure and holy seraphim evinced such reverence in the presence of Jehovah, with what profound awe and veneration should we, polluted and sinful creatures, presume to draw near to him!'[1]

While the seraphim covered their faces and feet, they used the remaining two wings to hover in the air, ever ready to dart away to serve their Lord. As they hovered before the Lord, they chanted, 'Holy, holy, holy is the LORD of hosts' (v. 3). The threefold repetition emphasizes that there is nothing about God that is more essential for us to know than that he is holy!

God's holiness means that he is of such a nature that he cannot be nonchalant about our sins; he must detest sin and pronounce and execute judgement upon it. Let us never doubt the love of God, but God never loves at the cost of denying his holiness. The love of God itself is a holy love. As great as the love of God for sinners is, God could not out of love pardon sinners without satisfying his holiness.

This brings us to the meaning of Jesus's death on the cross. The love of God was most certainly there, but the holiness of God was also there. Jesus was forsaken of God because God-forsakenness is what God's holiness demanded as the penalty for our sins (Matt. 27:46).

SHAKING AND SMOKE (V. 4)

Yet another indication of the sovereign authority of God came when 'the posts of the door were shaken' at the mere mention of his holiness and glory. We associate pillars with firmness and stability, but God is so powerful and great that he can make the unshakable to shake.

The smoke may suggest that God exercises his sovereignty in mysterious and unpredictable ways.

Isaiah saw himself (vv. 5–7)

When Isaiah saw the glory of the Lord, he saw himself and cried, 'Woe is me, for I am undone!' (v. 5).

He was broken up. He was especially aware of the foulness and vileness of his lips. Isaiah's speaking was probably cleaner than that of his contemporaries, but the standard of measurement was not others: it was God! With the holy God as his reference point, Isaiah realized how filthy he was. And his tongue was more filthy than anything else.

If we ever get a glimpse of the glory and majesty of our God, we, like Isaiah, will be made keenly aware of our own sinfulness, and our sinful tongues will probably come to mind first. When Isaiah saw his sinfulness and openly confessed it, the Lord cleansed him.

What did the Lord do? He sent one of the seraphim to touch Isaiah's lips with a hot coal from the altar. This conveyed to Isaiah that the Lord had indeed cleansed him of his sin.

The God of grace still promises forgiveness to all who will join Isaiah in confession of sin. The apostle John declares, 'If we confess our sins, He is faithful and just to forgive us our sins and to cleanse us from all unrighteousness' (1 John 1:9).

While we must ever insist on the holiness of God, we must never take it to mean that God is not gracious. He is both holy and gracious, and anyone who seeks to get us to choose only one of these attributes is asking us to separate friends! Here is the glory and the wonder of the Christian message. The sovereign, holy God of eternity is also a gracious God who forgives and cleanses us of our sins!

In his Gospel, the apostle John plainly indicates that it was none other than the Lord Jesus Christ whom Isaiah saw in his vision (John 12:37–41). Isaiah was humbled because he saw him in his glory. As we look into Scripture, we are also humbled as we see something of his glory. But there is another sight of Christ that produces humility in us—the sight of Christ in his humility.

Think for a moment about what it cost Christ to provide our salvation. What did it require of him? He had to stoop in humility; to strip himself of the trappings of glory and take unto himself our humanity, and in that humanity to render perfect obedience to the Law of God and receive in it the punishment our sins deserve.

The apostle Paul perfectly captured the redeeming work of Christ in these words: '[He] made Himself of no reputation, taking the form of a bondservant, and coming in the likeness of men. And being found in appearance as a man, He humbled Himself and became obedient to the point of death, even the death of the cross' (Phil. 2:7–8).

Paul did not share these words merely to inform the Philippians, but so that the Philippians would themselves follow the example of Christ. Before he began to detail the humility of Christ, Paul said to his readers, 'Let this mind be in you which was also in Christ Jesus …' (Phil. 2:5).

While we understand that revival is finally locked up in the sovereignty of God and cannot be produced by men, we can say that God is more likely to move upon people who are broken by their sins and humble before him. As we seek revival, let us join together in resolving that we will discard our pride and humble ourselves before God. In so doing, we will at least hoist our sails to catch the wind of heaven if and when it blows.

Reflect on these points

1. *Humility is to be the hallmark of Christians. However, while we enter God's family through the door of humility, we can, after entering, be filled with pride. No child of God is immune.*

2. *To ask how near we are to revival is to ask how near we are to humility. How often we think we know better than God! This is raw, undiluted pride!*

3. *God's holiness means that he must detest sin and pronounce and execute judgement upon it. Let us never doubt the love of God, but God never loves at the cost of denying his holiness.*

God's people pray

Oh, that You would rend the heavens! That You would come down! That the mountains might shake at Your presence—

As fire burns brushwood, As fire causes water to boil—To make Your name known to Your adversaries, That the nations may tremble at Your presence!

Isaiah 64:1–2

Thus says the LORD *of hosts: 'Peoples shall yet come, Inhabitants of many cities;*

'The inhabitants of one city shall go to another, saying, "Let us continue to go and pray before the LORD *…"'*

Zechariah 8:20–21

R evival is a time when God's people are moved to a higher level of prayer.

That remarkable theologian of revival, Jonathan Edwards, offered this observation about God's dealings with his people: 'When he is about to bestow some great blessing on his church, it is often his manner, in the first place, so to order things in his providence, as to show his church their need of it, and to bring them into distress for want of it, and so put them upon crying earnestly to him for it.'[1] Prayer is one of the indispensable means God uses to revive his people. There is no revival without it.

Many Scriptures connect revival and prayer. The best known of these is 2 Chronicles 7:14: '… if My people who are called by My name will humble themselves, and pray and seek My face, and turn from their wicked ways, then I will hear from heaven, and will forgive their sin and heal their land.' The psalmist Asaph prayed for revival in this way: 'Restore us, O God of hosts; Cause Your face to shine, And we shall be saved! (Ps. 80:7). He also prayed, 'Revive us, and we will call upon Your name' (Ps. 80:18). The prophecy of Isaiah includes a long prayer (Isa. 63:15–64:12) for spiritual renewal. In this prayer, the prophet begins by asking God to 'look down' (63:15) upon his people, but soon proceeds to this petition: 'come down!' (64:1).

The sharp question, then, is this: Are we praying for a mighty moving of God in our midst? If we want God to visit us and do his extraordinary work of revival, we must earnestly pray. It is as simple as that.

What kind of praying ought we to be doing? What kind of praying does God delight to hear and answer? What constitutes revival praying?

We must say that revival praying is:

Corporate prayer

In other words, God wants his people to gather together for prayer.

It is truly astonishing how little time is given to prayer in the average church these days. Many Christians seem to be far more concerned about prayer in the public schools than they are about prayer in church!

Jonathan Edwards, recognizing the crucial importance of corporate praying, wrote a treatise entitled *Humble Attempt to Promote Explicit and Visible Union of God's People in*

Extraordinary Prayer for Revival (the full title consisted of 187 words!). He was concerned to call Christians to prayer that would be explicit in agreement, united and extraordinary. In other words, he was calling upon the people of God to agree on the urgent need for praying for revival, to gather publicly to do so, and to do so in an extraordinary way, that is, to select special times for prayer and to give unusual time and effort to prayer.

Edwards had a scriptural basis for making this plea. In the prophecy of Zechariah, we find these words: 'Thus says the LORD of hosts: "Peoples shall yet come, inhabitants of many cities; the inhabitants of one city shall go to another, saying, 'Let us continue to go and pray before the LORD, and seek the LORD of hosts. I myself will go also'"' (Zech. 8:20–21).

Private prayer

God also wants his people to be praying privately for revival. Corporate prayer does not negate the need for private prayer.

Another quote from Edwards makes the point:

> There is no way that Christians in a private capacity can do so much to promote the work of God and advance the kingdom of Christ, as by prayer ... [I]f they have much of the spirit of grace and supplication, in this way they may have power with him who is infinite in power and has the government of the whole world. A poor man in his cottage may have a blessed influence all over the world.[2]

James, using the example of Elijah, assures us that 'the effective, fervent prayer of a righteous man avails much' (James 5:16). As we think about the wonderful things that God did in Elijah's time, we may very well find ourselves inclined to ask, 'Where now is the God of Elijah?' Someone has suggested that the answer to that question is this: 'He is waiting for Elijah to call on him.'

It is not enough, however, merely to say that we are to pray corporately and privately for revival. We must proceed to deal with:

The nature of corporate and private prayer

Here are several aspects mentioned by Scripture.

URGENT AND FERVENT

We are to pray urgently and fervently. This element stands out in Isaiah's revival prayer (Isa. 63:15–64:12). The King James Version uses the phrase 'behold, see, we beseech thee' to translate 'Indeed, please look …' in 64:9 of the New King James Version.

The word 'beseech' is much stronger than 'ask' or 'request'. Here is a word that has sweat on its brow and grime on its hands. It is a fervent and passionate word. It means to entreat, to implore, to beg, to plead. There is no easy-going moderation in this word.

Isaiah's prayer was urgent and fervent because it flowed from a keen sense that the people of God had lost much through sin and that only God himself could restore what had been lost.

He understood that the God who had worked on behalf of his people in former times was ready and willing to do so again.

The very same things are true of us. We also have lost much through sin. God can restore what has been lost, and he is ready and willing to do so. If we truly believe these things, we will have no trouble praying urgently and fervently.

PERSISTENT

We must also pray persistently. The people of whom Zechariah the prophet spoke would say, 'Let us continue to go and pray before the LORD' (Zech. 8:21). Isaiah speaks of giving God no rest until he makes his people 'a praise in the earth' (Isa. 62:7).

Some are always troubled by this. Why should we be persistent in prayer? If God knows we need something, why does he not just give it to us? The answer is that God wants us to be persistent for our own good. Benefits easily gained are not duly prized. That which has been won by toil and hardship is more apt to be guarded diligently, while that which comes easily is likely to be carelessly squandered away. In other words, if revival comes through persistent praying, we are likely to prize the benefits of revival and to guard them.

CONFIDENT

Finally, we are to pray confidently. When we pray for revival, we are praying for something that God has indeed promised to give his people from time to time. We need only to turn to Isaiah's prophecy again to find one such promise: 'For I will pour water on him who is thirsty, and floods on the dry ground; I will pour My Spirit on your descendants, and My blessing on your offspring ...' (Isa. 44:3).

The question is whether we are thirsty for God's reviving work. Are we thirsty enough to pray corporately and privately? Are we thirsty enough to pray fervently, persistently and confidently? The promise is for the thirsty. As long as we are content as we are, we shall never experience revival. May God help us to get thirsty.

Reflect on these points

1. *Prayer is one of the indispensable means God uses to revive his people. If we want God to do his work of revival, we must earnestly pray.*

2. *God wants his people to gather together for prayer. But many Christians seem to be far more concerned about prayer in the public schools than they are about prayer in church!*

3. *If God knows we need something, why does he not just give it to us? God wants us to be persistent for our own good. Benefits easily gained are not duly prized.*

4. *When we pray for revival, we are praying for something that God has promised to give his people from time to time.*

God's people repent

The word that came to Jeremiah from the LORD, *saying,*

'Stand in the gate of the LORD'*s house, and proclaim there this word, and say, "Hear the word of the* LORD, *all you of Judah who enter in at these gates to worship the* LORD!*"'*

Thus says the LORD *of hosts, the God of Israel: 'Amend your ways and your doings, and I will cause you to dwell in this place ...'*

Jeremiah 7:1–3

God's glorious work of revival is invariably characterized by God's people becoming broken over their sins and turning from them. There can be no revival apart from this. The Lord himself said to the people of Israel under Solomon: '... if My people who are called by My name will humble themselves, and pray and seek My face, and turn from their wicked ways, then I will hear from heaven, and will forgive their sin and heal their land' (2 Chr. 7:14).

Real repentance among God's people seems to be a very rare thing these days. The fact is that God's people are known more for what they turn toward than for what they turn from. It is not at all unusual to see professing Christians making sinful activities and attitudes part of their lives; it is rare to see them decisively casting such things aside. Brian H. Edwards was certainly correct to observe, 'It is a sad fact that in normal times Christians hold on to those things that revival will snatch away from them.'[1]

We are now face to face with the reason why there is such

little interest in revival. It is very costly! It is a kind of spiritual surgery in which sinful thoughts and deeds are removed.

What kind of spiritual surgery do you need? What is there in your life that needs to be removed? Is it an inclination to be critical and gossipy? Is it an addiction to pornography? Is it resentment toward someone? Is it a fondness for pleasure that consistently takes you out of public worship? Is it a love for money that is so strong that you even find yourself unwilling to support the work of the Lord financially?

Repentance is the spiritual knife that takes out of our hearts and lives the things that do not belong. Nothing is more unpopular these days! Surgical knives are never popular! Repentance has become so unpopular that many pastors never mention it. It drives the crowd away! Yet, although we may have changed our views on repentance, God has not changed his. He still insists upon it as the indispensable way to get sin out of our lives.

Jeremiah 7 gives us valuable insight into this matter of repentance. Here the prophet delivered his famous 'Temple Sermon'. He was commanded by the Lord to 'stand in the gate of the Lord's house' and preach to all those who came there to worship the Lord.

The fact that the people of Judah were coming to the house of the Lord would seem to suggest that Jeremiah's was a fool's errand. If the people were coming to worship the Lord, all would seem to be well. The sad fact is, however, that one can be in the house of the Lord on a regular basis and yet have a heart that is devoted to idols and is far from the Lord. The Lord Jesus himself warned about the danger of drawing nigh to God with our lips while our hearts are far from him (Mark 7:6–7).

The hearts of the people of Judah were far from the Lord. They were still going through the motions of worshipping him, but they were also worshipping their idols. They had not replaced the worship of God with the worship of idols; they merely allowed the two to co-exist.

The very same thing is going on today. Many think that, as long as they go to church on Sunday, they can live any way they want the rest of the week. They are trying to worship God and their idols.

The 'worshippers' in Judah must have been very surprised when they went to church on the day described in Jeremiah 7. There stood Jeremiah at the gate, preaching passionately! His message wasn't the smiling 'I'm okay, you're okay' variety. It wasn't a 'Have a nice day' message. He wasn't wearing a smiley button on his lapel.

His message was arresting and sobering. One phrase captured the essence of it: 'Amend your ways and your doings' (vv. 3, 5). It was a message of repentance. God was not impressed by the fact that the people were coming to his house; he was interested in the condition of their hearts.

Jeremiah's message called the people to revival. While the revival did not come, the prophet's message shows us that repentance is an essential part of revival. It also reveals the nature of real repentance.

Repentance deals with our ways

We have a tendency to judge the condition of our relationship with God on the basis of feelings. If we are emotionally moved in a service, we conclude that we are right with God.

Jeremiah's message fastened the attention of his hearers on the conduct of their lives. It did not for one moment matter how these people felt about themselves. They were not living according to the laws of God (vv. 5–6). They were responsible for keeping the Ten Commandments, yet Jeremiah here charged them with violating six of them (vv. 5–9).

Many today think the Ten Commandments have been diluted or withdrawn. Nothing could be farther from the truth. And if we want to know whether or not our ways are pleasing to the Lord, all we have to do is consult these commandments and not our feelings.

John the Baptist was called to prepare the way for the ministry of the Lord Jesus by delivering this message:

> Prepare the way of the Lord;
> Make His paths straight.
> Every valley shall be filled
> And every mountain and hill brought low;
> The crooked places shall be made straight
> And the rough ways smooth;
> And all flesh shall see the salvation of God.
>
> (Luke 3:4b–6; see also Isa.
> 40:3–4; Matt. 3:3; Mark 1:2–3)

When a king of ancient times desired to visit a particular

part of his kingdom, he would send an advance man to prepare the way. It was the responsibility of this man to make sure the king's journey was as pleasant and easy as possible. Low places in the road would be filled in. High places would be levelled. Crooked places in the road would be straightened out. It was all so the king could come to his subjects.

Let's face it: there are in our hearts low places of sin, high places of pride and arrogance, and crooked, devious ways. Revival means that the Lord comes to his people in a special way. His coming means low places must be filled in, the high places levelled and the crooked places straightened out.

In other words, there is no such thing as revival apart from repentance and brokenness. This is true heart work. We can engage in all kinds of work—publicity, promotions and so on—but all will be to no avail apart from preparation of our hearts. Let's remind ourselves of Samuel's words: '… prepare your hearts for the LORD, and serve Him only …' (I Sam. 7:3).

Repentance means change

The word 'amend' makes this plain (Jer. 7:3, 5). It means changing one's ways. We may picture it this way: when we are living in disobedience to the Lord, our faces are toward our sin and our backs toward the Lord. When we repent, we turn our backs on our sin and our faces toward the Lord and his will for our lives.

There is no true repentance where there is no change in a person's life. Some have the idea that they can continue to sin as long as they tell God they're sorry; but saying we are sorry without breaking with our sins is not genuine sorrow at all.

Real repentance recognizes God's standards for our behaviour, agrees with them, and is heartbroken over failing to adhere to them. It confesses with sincere sorrow and breaks with sin.

Real repentance always shows up in the life, and any repentance that does not show up in the life is a phoney repentance.

Repentance averts God's chastisement and brings his blessing

Jeremiah's temple sermon confronted the people of Judah with a choice. They could repent and receive God's blessings, or persist in their sins and bring calamity upon themselves.

The Lord set the possibility of blessing before the people in these words: 'Amend your ways and your doings, and I will cause you to dwell in this place' (vv. 3, 7). In other words, he promised stability and security to his people if they would repent; but they were far from repentance. They felt no shame over their behaviour. When sin was mentioned, they passed it off as something that was of no importance. They believed that the outward form of religion (going to the temple and observing its rituals) was more than enough to cancel their sins and gain the favour of God.

They were dreadfully mistaken. During Samuel's time, their forefathers had made the very same mistake. They had thought God was obligated to bless and keep them as long as they kept up the outward display of religion. On the basis of this belief, they carried the ark of the covenant into battle against the Philistines. There they discovered how mistaken they were. The ark of God was taken and the tabernacle at Shiloh was apparently demolished (1 Sam. 4:1–11).

It has often been said that those who refuse to learn from history are doomed to repeat it. The people of Jeremiah's generation had not learned from the Shiloh chapter in their history, and God was now telling them that they must genuinely repent or suffer a similar calamity. Through his prophet, he said of the temple, '… therefore I will do to the house which is called by My name, in which you trust, and to this place which I gave to you and your fathers, as I have done to Shiloh' (v. 14).

The people refused to repent, and the Lord did exactly as he promised. The Babylonians came against Judah, completely destroyed the temple and the city of Jerusalem, and carried most of Judah's citizens into captivity.

We remind ourselves of the people of Judah, not because we have some unusual interest in ancient history, but rather because we face the very same choice that they faced. We may enjoy God's blessings or we may experience his chastisement. Repentance brings the former; refusal to repent, the latter.

Reflect on these points

1. *Real repentance among God's people seems to be very rare these days. God's people are known more for what they turn toward than for what they turn from.*

2. *There is no such thing as revival apart from repentance*

and brokenness. Revival is very costly—a kind of spiritual surgery in which sinful thoughts and deeds are removed. What kind of spiritual surgery do you need?

3. *Some have the idea that they can continue to sin as long as they tell God they're sorry; but real repentance recognizes God's standards for our behaviour, agrees with them, and is heartbroken over failing to adhere to them.*

God's people value God's Word

Then Hilkiah the high priest said to Shaphan the scribe, 'I have found the Book of the Law in the house of the LORD.' And Hilkiah gave the book to Shaphan, and he read it ...

Then Shaphan the scribe showed the king, saying, 'Hilkiah the priest has given me a book.' And Shaphan read it before the king.

Now it happened, when the king heard the words of the Book of the Law, that he tore his clothes ...

2 Kings 22:8, 10–11

Now all the people gathered together as one man in the open square that was in front of the Water Gate; and they told Ezra the scribe to bring the Book of the Law of Moses, which the LORD had commanded Israel.

So Ezra the priest brought the Law before the assembly of men and women and all who could hear with understanding ...

Then he read from it in the open square ...

Nehemiah 8:1–3

These two passages describe revivals that occurred among the people of God. In the first of these, the focus is on the Word of God. In the second, the emphasis is on the preaching of God's Word. Both the Word and the preaching of the Word are recovered and appreciated when revival comes.

Josiah: A new appreciation of God's Word (2 Kings 22:1–20)

When Josiah came to the throne of Judah at the tender age of eight, he found wretched conditions. His father, Amon, had plunged the nation into the most revolting idolatry imaginable (2 Kings 21:19–26).

While Josiah was still a very young man, he realized that the idolatry his father had pursued was wrong and must be stopped. So, in the twelfth year of his reign, he began a campaign to purge idols from the nation (2 Chr. 34:3–7). Six years later, he called for the temple of the Lord to be repaired. We should not be surprised at this. The temple always fell into a state of disrepair in times of idolatry.

It was in the course of the renovation that 'the Book of the Law' was discovered (2 Kings 22:8). In all likelihood, it was the book of Deuteronomy.

We cannot say how long the nation had been deprived of the message of this book, but we can say that, during that time, the nation was missing a most important and vital message. The book of Deuteronomy lays out the importance of God's people obeying him. It tells of the blessings that God sends upon an obedient people and the devastating judgement he sends upon those who refuse to obey.

We may very well find ourselves marvelling as we read this account. How could the people of Judah have lost the very Word on which their nation was founded and by which it was framed?

The answer, of course, is that the nation had shifted from its foundation. It had forsaken God's covenant and embraced worthless idols. When a nation or an individual begins to move away from God, the Bible becomes a source of irritation. Its very presence is like a sharp stick in the eye.

The Bible is the bulwark against false religion and idolatry. Those who want to promote the false must, of necessity, dispense with the true. We can well imagine, therefore, the idolatrous kings who preceded Josiah making a concentrated effort to destroy every copy of the Word of God.

It's easy enough for us to see the problem of those days. The kings and the people of Judah themselves did not properly prize the Word of God. They were anxious to destroy it. It is much more difficult for us to see our own failures to adequately prize the Bible.

There is more than one way to lose the Bible. We have Bibles everywhere. There does not appear to be much chance of us losing it in the way that it was lost in Josiah's day. But we can lose it in another way: we can lose its message even while we hold it in our hands.

There are many signs that this is happening. We have the Bible, but we are ignoring large portions of it. We tend to look right past those passages that talk about sin, holiness, repentance and coming judgement. There is even an increasing tendency to disregard the Bible's message about the cross of Christ being the only possible way of salvation. We are much more comfortable looking for passages that help us cope with the here and now.

After Hilkiah the priest found the book of Deuteronomy, Shaphan the scribe carried it to Josiah and read it to him (2 Kings 22:10).

The king could have said something like this: 'There's

no reason for us to be concerned. This is a very old book. It is outdated. It has no relevance for us.' Or he could have said something along these lines: 'These are modern and sophisticated times. No one believes like that any more.' Instead, he 'tore his clothes' (v. 11). By doing so, he outwardly demonstrated that his heart was torn with sorrow and grief over the failure of his nation to adhere to what was written in this book. Huldah the prophetess would later note that Josiah had received the Word of God with a tender heart and had humbled himself before the Lord (v. 19).

A tender heart is one that is soft rather than hard. It is a heart that is capable of receiving an impression. If a seal or stamp is pressed against a stone, no impression is left, but if it is pressed against soft wax, an indelible impression remains. Josiah's heart had been like soft wax when the book of Deuteronomy was pressed against it.

Josiah's eager response to the Book of the Law reflects how we are to respond to the message of God's Word (see Acts 17:11; 1 Thes. 2:13; James 1:21).

Ezra: A new appreciation for the preaching of God's Word (Neh. 8:1–12)

We cannot truly appreciate God's Word without appreciating the primary means God has appointed for delivering it to his people.

Nehemiah 8 gives us a gripping picture of God's people prizing the preaching of his Word in a time of revival. The people of Israel were back in their own land after years of captivity in Babylon. They had been back long enough to accomplish a good many things, but one thing they had failed to accomplish: they had failed to give attention to the Scriptures.

Nehemiah had led the people of Jerusalem to rebuild the walls of their city. After this task was completed, he turned his attention to an even more formidable task, namely, bringing true spiritual renewal.

The plan for renewal called for Ezra to conduct a systematic exposition of God's Word. This was necessary because the Law of Moses was originally written in Hebrew and the people now spoke Aramaic. Furthermore, in the years after their return from captivity, they had been preoccupied with rebuilding their homes, the temple and the city walls.

So a time was selected, a high platform was built and assistants for Ezra were enlisted. The idea was for Ezra to read a passage and for these assistants to translate, explain and apply it. These assistants, thirteen in number, would be needed because the number anticipated would be too large for Ezra to be heard.

Oftentimes, leaders have diligently planned only to be disappointed by the response. This was not the case for Ezra. The people turned out in robust numbers and 'told Ezra the scribe to bring the Book of the Law of Moses, which the LORD had commanded Israel' (Neh. 8:1).

The eagerness of the people for the Word was demonstrated by their standing in reverence when Ezra opened the book and their cry of 'Amen, Amen!' in response to Ezra's opening words (vv. 5–6). It is also apparent in these words: 'And they bowed their heads and worshiped the LORD with their faces to the ground' (v. 6).

This intense interest was rewarded with several hours ('from morning until midday', v. 3) of sustained teaching from the Word of God, which led both to tears of sorrow (v. 9) and profound joy (vv. 10–12). The sorrow was fitting in that they had sinned against the Lord; the joy, in that the Lord was sufficient for their sins.

It was a time of revival, and it was ignited by the preaching of God's Word. There has never been a revival without God's people falling in love again with biblical preaching.

If interest in preaching is an indication of revival, we surely have to realize that the church is not now experiencing revival. No matter where we turn, pastors and churches seem to be fleeing from the preaching of the Word of God. The famine prophesied by Amos is much among us (Amos 8:11).

The flight from biblical preaching takes more than one form. Sometimes, it takes the form of referring to the music portion of our services as the 'worship' time and those who lead the music as 'worship leaders'. The clear implication, of course, is that preaching, whatever it may be, is not part of worship! This is a substantial departure from the sentiment of Martin Luther, who wrote, 'The highest worship of God is the preaching of the Word.'[1]

Oftentimes, the flight manifests itself by replacing preaching altogether with musicals and dramas. In the United States, it has become commonplace for churches not to have Sunday evening services at all. Among those churches that retain the services, there is a general willingness to quickly lay them aside for almost any reason, including, amazingly enough, the viewing of the Super Bowl each February!

Yet another form is not as apparent but every bit as dangerous. It is the flight that takes place even when the preacher stands in the pulpit. The fact that someone stands to preach does not mean that true preaching will be done! Multitudes of preachers have abandoned the preaching of the holiness of God, the awful reality of sin, the certainty of divine judgement, the sufficiency and finality of Christ and the crucial importance of repentance. The Bible, which has redemption through Christ as its theme, has now become a handbook with principles for comfortable living, with barely any mention of Christ at all! The supreme concern of the modern-day pulpit is how to get people happily through the week instead of safely into eternity!

There is no surprise here. Times of declension always turn things upside down, including the place of preaching. But revival turns them right side up! How we need revival!

Reflect on these points

1. When a nation or an individual begins to move away from God, the Bible becomes a source of irritation. Its very presence is like a sharp stick in the eye.

2. *We have the Bible, but we are ignoring large portions of it. We are much more comfortable looking for passages that help us cope with the here and now.*

3. *We cannot truly appreciate God's Word without appreciating the primary means God has appointed for delivering it to his people: preaching.*

4. *If interest in preaching is an indication of revival, we surely have to realize that the church is not now experiencing revival. The famine prophesied by Amos is among us.*

God's people
prize his house
and his gospel

In the first year of his reign, in the first month, he [Hezekiah] opened the doors of the house of the LORD and repaired them.

Then he brought in the priests and the Levites, and gathered them in the East Square, and said to them: 'Hear me, Levites! Now sanctify yourselves, sanctify the house of the LORD God of your fathers, and carry out the rubbish from the holy place ...'

2 Chronicles 29:3–5

And Hezekiah sent to all Israel and Judah, and also wrote letters to Ephraim and Manasseh, that they should come to the house of the LORD at Jerusalem, to keep the Passover to the LORD God of Israel ...

2 Chronicles 30:1

When Hezekiah came to the throne, the nation of Judah was in a supreme mess. Enemies had been threatening the nation's existence (2 Chr. 28:16–18, 20), many of her citizens had either been killed or deported (29:9) and the temple of the Lord had been closed (29:7).

It was all due to the extreme wickedness of Hezekiah's father, Ahaz. Second Chronicles 28:19 says, 'For the LORD brought Judah low because of Ahaz king of Israel, for he had encouraged moral decline in Judah and had been continually unfaithful to the LORD.'

Hezekiah and the temple: Prizing God's house (29:3–19)

Hezekiah wasted no time in addressing the situation, focusing first on cleansing the temple of the Lord. The phrase 'the house of the LORD' appears eleven times in 2 Chronicles 29. We also find references in this chapter to the holy place, the dwelling place of the Lord, the temple of the Lord, the vestibule of the Lord and the sanctuary. It is clear that the focus is on God's house.

This house, built by King Solomon, was originally very beautiful and glorious, but Hezekiah found it in a very pathetic and sorrowful state. His father Ahaz had cut up the sacred articles of the house and had closed its doors (28:24).

A first-class idolater, Ahaz had no interest in or use for the house of the Lord. Hezekiah was different. The Lord of grace had put it in his heart to 'make a covenant with the LORD God of Israel' (29:10). That grace enabled Hezekiah to see that the troubles of his kingdom were due to the wrath of God, and the wrath of God was due to the leaders and people neglecting the Lord and his house. Hezekiah put it in these words: '... our fathers have trespassed and done evil in the eyes of the LORD our God; they have forsaken Him, have turned their faces away from the dwelling place of the LORD, and turned their backs on Him' (29:6).

So Hezekiah assembled the Levites (the men who were responsible for the oversight and upkeep of the temple) and commanded them to thoroughly clean the temple. His words 'do not be negligent now' (v. 11) amounted to a sharp rebuke to them for being negligent in the past.

The Levites took Hezekiah's charge to heart and set to work. Starting in the 'inner part of the house of the LORD', they carried out 'all the debris' and dumped it in the Brook Kidron (v. 16), where in the rainy season it would be swept away and deposited in the Dead Sea. They then gave themselves to sanctifying the house of the Lord (vv. 17–19).

Their first look at all the dirt and filth in the temple must have caused them to feel overwhelmed, but they tackled the job and finished it in sixteen days.

With everything back in order, sacrifices were resumed (vv. 20–27) and the congregation worshipped (vv. 28–30). The author summarizes it all by saying, 'So the service of the house of the LORD was set in order. Then Hezekiah and all the people rejoiced that God had prepared the people, since the events took place so suddenly' (vv. 35b–36).

What had happened? Revival had come and had brought with it a new interest in and devotion to the Lord's house.

Does this have anything to do with us? It does. The temple of the Lord in Hezekiah's time was the place of worship, and the revival meant the restoration of worship. Part of the glory of revival is that it causes God's people to fall in love again with public worship in God's house. Revival causes the saints to see God's house for what it is: a God-meeting, need-meeting, truth-meeting, family-meeting place.

Do we need public worship in God's house? We certainly do. But God's people can get terribly careless and casual about the house of God. A thousand excuses are ready at hand.

In my book *They Echoed the Voice of God*, I shared these words:

It has become very difficult for spiritual leaders to … gather the people … Many church leaders have had so little success and so much disappointment in trying to gather the people that they have long since given up even trying. Others have determined that the only way the church can gather a party-mad people is by throwing a bigger party! Someone has observed that it is virtually impossible to get people together when God is the only attraction!

Church people always say to church leaders, 'You must pick a convenient time to gather the people.' And God says to church people, 'You must lay aside those things that make the time inconvenient.'[1]

Hezekiah and the Passover: Prizing the gospel (30:1–5; see also 35:1–19)

Hezekiah's observance of the Passover speaks to us about an element that is present in every revival, that is, recovering high esteem for the gospel of Christ. The Passover was specifically designed by God to point the people of the Old Testament to the coming of the Lord Jesus Christ. When the Passover was lost, it could only mean that faith in the promised Christ was slipping. When the Passover was restored, faith in Christ was coming back.

THE HISTORICAL EVENT

The Passover takes us back to that time when Moses and the people of Israel were in bondage in Egypt. The Lord had sent nine plagues upon Pharaoh and the Egyptians. Although these plagues were devastating in nature, Pharaoh refused to release the Israelites. The stage was now set for the tenth and final plague: God's death angel taking the lives of the firstborn in the land of Egypt (Exod. 11:4–6).

We must be careful to note that God's death sentence against the firstborn included all those in the land of Egypt. Even the firstborn of the people of Israel would have been slain had it not been for the special provision God made for his people: that '… every man shall take for himself a lamb …' (Exod. 12:3).

Each Israelite was to stay in his or her house marked with the blood. When the death angel saw that blood, he would pass over their houses, that is, he would not stop to execute the sentence of death. The lambs would have died in their stead.

God did just as he promised. All the firstborn of Egypt died (Exod. 12:29–30), but the people of Israel were passed over. The lamb made the difference!

THE SPIRITUAL PICTURE

The Passover will seem to us to be nothing more than a strange piece of history if we do not keep in mind that Christ is our Passover (1 Cor. 5:7). Like Israel of old, we are all sinners by nature and under the sentence of God's wrath (John 3:36; Eph. 2:3).

We must understand that God is holy. That means that he himself is free from sin. But it also means that he cannot ignore the sins of his creatures. His holy nature requires him to judge sin. For him to refuse to do so would be to deny his holy nature. This he cannot do. Furthermore, God's holy nature requires him to separate himself from the sinner and his or her sin. This, then, is the wrath of God—separation from God for ever and active punishment for sin. The Bible refers to the final instalment of the wrath of God as hell, the lake of fire and eternal destruction.

If that were the whole story, we would be the most pathetic creatures imaginable, but there is more. The same God whose holiness calls from him the utmost wrath against sin is also kind, gracious and loving. This loving nature compels him to forgive sinners.

The sharp, piercing question of the ages, the dilemma that dwarfs and surpasses all others, was this: How could God at one and the same time pour out his eternal wrath on sinners, thus satisfying his holy nature, and let those same sinners go free, thus satisfying his gracious nature?

The wisdom of God found the answer: the Lord Jesus Christ and his death on the cross. Jesus went to that cross for the express purpose of receiving the wrath of God in the place of sinners. Is the very essence of the wrath of God being separated or abandoned by God? On the cross, Jesus cried out, 'My God, My God, why have You forsaken Me?' (Matt. 27:46).

Jesus did not suffer the wrath of God for his own sins, because he had no sins (1 John 3:5). He was the Lamb without spot or blemish (1 Peter 1:19). He went to the cross to receive wrath for others.

But if our sins deserve an eternity of separation from God,

how could Jesus receive that wrath in the few hours that he was on the cross? Here we are in the area of infinities and immensities. We will never be able to understand this in this life. We can only say that Jesus was no ordinary human being; he was God in human flesh. As God, he was an infinite person. As an infinite person, therefore, he could receive in a finite amount of time an infinite amount of wrath!

The good news about the wrath of God is this: the same holy nature of God that requires him to pour out his wrath on sinners will not allow him to pour out wrath twice on the same sinner. His holiness requires that the penalty for sin only be paid once. If Jesus paid it, all those who take refuge in him, who avail themselves of his redeeming death, who repent of their sins and believe in him, will never have to experience the wrath of God themselves. If Jesus received God's wrath for me, there is no wrath for me to receive! Jesus is my Passover. God in wrath passes over me, because the wrath has been poured out on him.

The blood of Christ has to be individually applied. If we want God to pass over us and not visit us in judgement, we must appropriate the redeeming work of Christ by faith. It is not enough to know that Jesus died on the cross; we must personally trust in what he did there. The Israelites were not saved from death merely because they were born Israelites, and we are not saved from eternal wrath because we have been born into a Christian family or because we have been brought up to go to church.

As we have already indicated, the apostle Paul calls Christ 'our Passover' (1 Cor. 5:7). So he is. We have all we need in Christ to escape the judgement of God.

The gospel is such a glorious message that we can only be astonished and stupefied that so much of the professing church has laid it aside to proclaim things that pertain only to living successfully in this world. How can such a thing happen? The answer is that people focus on this life because eternity does not weigh on them. Brian H. Edwards declares, 'The terrifying thing about modern man is that he no longer feels afraid, or feels anything about eternity.'[2]

Revival changes the blind preoccupation and the feverish fascination with the things of this world. Those things are seen to be what they are—trivial and passing—and eternity becomes the pressing issue. In times of revival, people realize the truth of the words of Jesus: 'For what profit is it to a man if he gains the whole world, and loses his own soul? Or what will a man give in exchange for his soul?' (Matt. 16:26).

Brian H. Edwards observes, 'Revival does not persuade the world that the Christian faith is *fun*, but that it is *essential*' (his italics).[3]

In times of revival, people become urgently concerned about leaving this life and standing in the presence of the holy God. They understand Revelation 6:15–17, which describes sinners as desiring to be covered by the rocks and mountains so that they will not have to face God.

The solemn reality of their sins and the enormous reality

of meeting God in their sin creates within them a sense of desperation. Then they learn about the Lord Jesus and his death on the cross. By the power of God's Spirit, they understand the wrath-receiving nature of that death. And they flee to Christ and take refuge in him. No need now for rocks and mountains to hide them from God's wrath; they are hidden in a far more secure refuge.

Tell me how terrible the wrath of God is to you, and I will tell you how precious the gospel is to you. If the former is awesomely dreadful, the latter is unspeakably glorious.

In normal times, we labour—often unsuccessfully, it seems—to make these things clear. But revival is not normal, and it does not come without causing sinners to tremble at the wrath of God and multitudes to flee to Christ. And it does not come without causing Christians to fall in love again with the gospel of Christ.

Reflect on these points

1. *Revival causes God's people to fall in love again with public worship in God's house, to see God's house for what it is: a God-meeting, need-meeting, truth-meeting, family-meeting place.*

2. *God's people can get careless and casual about the house of God. A thousand excuses are ready at hand.*

3. *How is it that much of the professing church has laid aside the glorious message of the gospel to proclaim things that pertain only to living successfully in this world? Because eternity does not weigh on them.*

4. *Revival changes the preoccupation and fascination with the things of this world. Those things are seen to be what they are—trivial and passing—and eternity becomes the pressing issue.*

God's people are reconciled with one another

Again the word of the LORD *came to me, saying,*

'As for you, son of man, take a stick for yourself and write on it: "For Judah and for the children of Israel, his companions." Then take another stick and write on it, "For Joseph, the stick of Ephraim, and for all the house of Israel, his companions."

'Then join them one to another for yourself into one stick, and they will become one in your hand. And when the children of your people speak to you, saying, "Will you not show us what you mean by these?" ...

'Then say to them, "Thus says the Lord GOD: 'Surely I will take the children of Israel from among the nations, wherever they have gone, and will gather them from every side and bring them into their own land;

'And I will make them one nation in the land, on the mountains of Israel; and one king shall be king over them all; they shall no longer be two nations, nor shall they ever be divided into two kingdoms again.'"'

Ezekiel 37:15–17, 21–22

After the death of King Solomon, the nation of Israel divided into two kingdoms. Ten tribes rebelled against Solomon's son, King Rehoboam, installed Jeroboam as their king and retained the name 'Israel'. The remaining two tribes, Judah and Benjamin, became known as the kingdom of Judah. This kingdom continued to be ruled by the descendants of King David.

Each of these two kingdoms finally went into captivity. The kingdom of Israel was taken captive by the Assyrians in 722 BC;

the kingdom of Judah by the Babylonians in 586 BC. The Assyrian Empire was itself eventually conquered and displaced by the Babylonian Empire. So when the people of Judah were taken to Babylon, they found many citizens of Israel already there.

Ezekiel was a priest of Judah who was exiled to Babylon in 597 BC (we must keep in mind that there were a couple of preliminary deportations of Judah's citizens to Babylon before the big one in 586 BC). There in Babylon, Ezekiel was called by God to prophesy to his fellow-captives from both Israel and Judah, and there, by the good grace of God, those fellow-captives experienced true revival (see Ps. 126:1–3). They broke with their idols and turned back to the Lord.

One stick

One of the major things that happened during this in-captivity revival was that the people from the two kingdoms, Israel and Judah, were reconciled to one another. Their hearts were turned towards one another and away from the animosity and hostility that had existed for years.

This reconciliation was so complete that the citizens of the two kingdoms emerged from captivity, not as two nations, but as one. Ezekiel was to demonstrate this to his hearers by using two sticks, one of which was to be labelled 'Judah', and the other, 'Ephraim' or 'Israel' (Ezek. 37:15–16). He was then to join the two sticks in his hand as one (v. 17).

When the people asked him to explain the two sticks, Ezekiel was to deliver this promise from God: '… I will make them one nation in the land, on the mountains of Israel; and one king shall be king over them all; they shall no longer be two nations, nor shall they ever be divided into two kingdoms again' (v. 22). God had made this same prophecy earlier through Isaiah (Isa. 11:13), Jeremiah (Jer. 3:18) and Hosea (Hosea 1:11).

In captivity, then, the citizens of Israel and Judah were restored in their relationship to God, and they were also restored in their relationship to one another, because the former always entails the latter. We are face to face, then, with this truth: we cannot be rightly related to God if we are wrongly related to one another.

There has never been a revival without individual Christians being reconciled to those with whom they have been at odds. God will not bypass resentment and bitterness to bestow his wonderful blessing of revival; revival requires us to deal with such things.

And there seems to be plenty for us to deal with. Almost every church has been hampered at one time or another by unresolved tensions and conflicts. Sometimes tensions exist between church staff members, sometimes between pastors and members, and sometimes between members and members. Sadly enough, the cause of such problems is often very trivial.

Tensions and conflicts are so common in our churches that someone was compelled to write,

> To live above with saints we love,
> Oh, that will be glory;
> But to live below with saints we know—
> That's a different story.
>
> (Anon.)

One tree

Reconciliation between Christians is inevitable in times of revival because of that truth we noted in an earlier chapter: revival causes God's people to prize the gospel of Christ. And the gospel is all about reconciliation.

We might say that revival calls God's people to exalt a tree—Calvary's tree (the cross of Christ!).

The apostle Paul found it necessary often to call believers to unity in Christ (Eph. 4:1–6: Phil. 2:1–11; 4:2; Col. 3:12–15). He always bathed every Christian responsibility in Calvary's love. In his letter to the Ephesians, he wrote, 'And be kind to one another, tenderhearted, forgiving one another, even as God in Christ forgave you' (Eph. 4:32).

The cross of Calvary takes every hiding place away from those who refuse to forgive. If we refuse to forgive someone because he or she doesn't deserve it, we must look at Calvary's love. The Lord Jesus Christ did not come and die for us because we were deserving; he came and died for us while we were ungodly and undeserving (Rom. 5:6–8).

If we refuse to forgive because of the serious nature of the offence perpetrated against us, we must look again at Calvary's love. No greater offence could be perpetrated than that which sinners have committed against God. And yet God took our humanity and in that humanity went to the cross. There he cried, 'Father, forgive them …' (Luke 23:34).

If we refuse to forgive because the person who has offended us seems to be vile and detestable in our eyes, we must look to the cross. There God made a way of forgiveness for the most vile and despicable creatures imaginable, those who had thumbed their noses at his Law and nailed the very Son of God to the cross.

If we refuse to forgive because we are waiting for the other person to take the first step, we must look at Calvary's love. Redemption is all about God taking the first step and all the steps. There would be no redemption without that because guilty sinners have neither the inclination nor the ability to take the first step toward God.

If we refuse to forgive because it might shatter our pride by requiring us to admit that we are wrong, we must look to Calvary. There the Lord, who had no pride and never did anything wrong, voluntarily stooped in humility and took upon himself our wrongs.

The cross of Christ is ever the antidote for a sour disposition and an unforgiving spirit. If we persist in such things, we only give evidence that we have not studied thoroughly and deeply its lessons.

How are we to avoid a sour, critical disposition? How can we keep our relationship with our brothers and sisters in good repair? How can we avoid getting into a situation in which we need to resolve tension and conflict? Paul urges us to let the peace of God rule in our hearts (Col. 3:15).

The Christian's purchased possession is peace. Peace with God and peace within from the guilt and condemnation of sin were purchased for all believers by the redeeming death of Christ on the cross.

Living at peace with others comes as we realize who we are in Christ Jesus. The more we reflect on what he has done for us, the more we shall find his peace dominating and controlling our lives. And the more peace controls us, the fewer tensions there will be in our relationships with others.

Reflect on these points

1. *We cannot be rightly related to God if we are wrongly related to one another. And God will not bypass resentment and bitterness to bestow his wonderful blessing of revival; revival requires us to deal with such things.*

2. *Reconciliation between Christians is inevitable in times of revival because revival causes God's people to prize the gospel of Christ. And the gospel is all about reconciliation.*

3. *The cross of Calvary takes every hiding place away from those who refuse to forgive. If we persist in such things, we only give evidence that we have not studied thoroughly and deeply its lessons.*

The hopeful plea of a hopeful heart

Return, O Lord!

   How long?

   And have compassion on Your servants.

Oh, satisfy us early with Your mercy,

   That we may rejoice and be glad all our days!

Make us glad according to the days in

      which You have afflicted us,

   The years in which we have seen evil.

Let Your work appear to Your servants,

   And Your glory to their children.

And let the beauty of the Lord our God be upon us,

   And establish the work of our hands for us;

   Yes, establish the work of our hands.

                                   Psalm 90:13–17

We must sadly admit that the battle for revival is often lost before it ever begins. Why? Because God's people do not really desire revival. The reason is that they are comfortable the way they are.

This calls to mind the citizens of Gadara who, after Jesus had delivered the demon-possessed man who was terrorizing their community, asked Jesus to leave! They were afraid that this powerful Jesus who had so changed the demoniac in their midst would insist on changing them. They were more comfortable living with the demoniac than they would be living with Jesus. So he had to go (Mark 5:15–17)!

Psalm 90 was written by Moses, a man who did not care about his comfort being disturbed. Verses 13 to 17 express a fervent yearning for God to bless his people. James Montgomery Boice refers to them as 'an appeal to God for an outpouring of his grace'.[1]

In this psalm, Moses reflected on the brevity of life (vv. 5–6, 10, 12). As he brought it to a conclusion, he seemed to realize that there was only a limited amount of time for God to do something of an extraordinary nature. So he prayed to that end.

Moses was a man who saw God do several extraordinary things, but that did not keep him from longing to see God work yet again. Many of us would have to admit that we have seen little or nothing of an extraordinary nature. If Moses, with all he had seen, longed for God to do an extraordinary work, how much more should those of us who have seen little or nothing be longing for this kind of thing?

Moses' prayer contains four petitions that have particular relevance for the whole matter of revival. May God help us to know the yearning of Moses' heart and to make his petitions ours!

Let your work appear to your servants (v. 16)

We know that God has many works. Here are a few:

- regeneration, in which he turns sinners to himself
- sanctification, in which he matures and grows those whom he regenerates

- providence, in which he governs all things according to his purposes
- revival, in which he brings his people back to spiritual vigour.

Let's not try to decide which of God's works the psalmist had in mind. Let's rather understand him to be praying along these lines:

- 'Let your work of regeneration appear' by saving those who seem to be too hard of heart to be saved. Let it appear by saving those for whom your people have prayed for many years. Let it appear by saving those who keep up the outward form of religion but know nothing of the reality of it.
- 'Let your work of sanctification appear' by enabling us to win victories over sin, by giving us a keener appetite for your Word, your worship and the work of your kingdom. Let it appear by causing us to delight less and less in the temporal things and more and more in eternal things.
- 'Let your work of providence appear' by letting us know that you have a plan and purpose in all the things that you allow to come our way, and by helping us to trust in your kind purpose even when we do not understand it.
- 'Let your work of revival appear' by making us realize that you are in our midst to draw us away from sin and self and to restore us to spiritual vibrancy.

God is always at work in the lives of his people and in the world around them, but we often have difficulty discerning his work. In times of revival, the scales fall from our eyes and we see the wonderful works of God and rejoice in them.

Let your glory appear to our children (v. 16)

Nothing is more important to the child of God than that his or her own children come to the knowledge of the Lord. But many of God's people carry very heavy hearts at this point. They brought their children up in the things of God, only to see them turn away. All their prayers and persuasive arguments seem to be of no avail.

Every believer with unbelieving children should be praying earnestly for revival because in times of revival, God abundantly answers this petition. Revivals have invariably included God moving in mighty power upon young people, causing them to see the sober reality of eternity and the utter folly of living for this world.

Let your beauty be upon us (v. 17)

God has already beautified his people with salvation. On the basis of the redeeming work of Christ, he has forgiven them their sins and clothed them in the righteousness of Christ.

What, then, was the psalmist asking with this petition? He was asking God to so move in the hearts of his people that they would make it known that they had been saved. He was asking God to enable his people to live in such a way that they displayed or demonstrated the beauty of salvation.

How is the beauty of salvation seen in the people of God? It is seen in their ...

- faithfulness to their commitments
- kindness in all they say and do
- refusal to take offence even in the face of extreme provocation
- willingness to forgive when they are wronged.

We might say that the beauty of salvation is seen in God's people when they live holy lives, that is, when they live in obedience to God's Word and do so in a glad and winsome way.

Revival never fails to bring beauty back to the people of God, who have been soiled by sin and stained by the world.

Establish the work of our hands (v. 17)

With this petition, we should understand the psalmist to be asking God to make the work of his people so excellent and effective that it would long endure after they were gone; to so bless their work that it would continue to bear fruit; to make their work of such a nature that it would make a lasting impression on those who came after them, even to the point that they also would want to faithfully serve the Lord.

The psalmist's petitions present us with a very stiff and challenging test. Do we really want revival? Do we long for God to make his work manifest? Do we yearn for him to show himself to our children? Do we fervently desire that his beauty should be displayed in our lives? Do we intensely long for him to make our work for him linger long after we are gone?

God's people easily pay lip-service to the subject of revival. Let a pastor stand before his people and say 'We need revival', and there will be nods of agreement and even an 'Amen' or two. But we often desire revival for the wrong reasons. Revival brings with it many positive benefits for society. It sweeps out many problems and ills and brings stability and tranquillity. It is very easy, therefore, for us to desire revival because we want the positive benefits; we want life to be more comfortable and pleasant.

The true motive for revival is to see God glorified. That is the reason why we should yearn for it and pray for it. A quick glance at the petitions of the psalmist is all it takes to see that the things for which he asked all bring glory to God.

Reflect on these points

1. *The battle for revival is often lost before it begins, because God's people do not really desire it. They are comfortable the way they are.*

2. *God is always at work in the lives of his people and in the world, but we often have difficulty discerning his work. In times of revival, we see his wonderful works and rejoice in them.*

3. *Every believer with unbelieving children should be praying earnestly for revival because in times of revival, God abundantly answers this petition.*

4. *Do we really want revival? The true motive for revival is to see God glorified. That is why we should yearn for it and pray for it.*

Endnotes

Introduction

1 J. I. Packer, *A Quest for Godliness* (Wheaton, IL: Crossway, 1990), p. 36.

2 Eifion Evans, 'Preaching and Revival', *Banner of Truth*, 87 (1970), p. 11.

3 Brian H. Edwards, *Revival! A People Saturated with God* (Darlington: Evangelical Press, 1990), p. 29.

Ch. 2 God has expectations for his people

1 Matthew Henry, *Matthew Henry's Commentary*, vol. i ([n.p.] Fleming H. Revell [n.d.]), p. 768.

2 Isaac Watts, 'When I Survey the Wondrous Cross'.

3 Henry, *Commentary*, p. 768.

Ch. 3 God's people have every reason to live up to his expectations

1 Charles R. Erdman, *The Epistles of Paul to the Colossians and to Philemon* (Philadelphia: Westminster Press, 1933), p. 43.

2 Cited in Geoffrey B. Wilson, *Colossians and Philemon: A Digest of Reformed Comment* (Edinburgh: Banner of Truth, 1980), p. 26.

3 John Newton, 'Amazing Grace'.

4 Richard Lenski, *The Interpretation of St Paul's Epistles to the Colossians, to the Thessalonians, to Timothy, to Titus and to Philemon* (Minneapolis: Augsburg Publishing, 1964), p. 39.

Ch. 4 God's people sometimes backslide

1 Richard Owen Roberts, *Revival* (Wheaton, IL: Tyndale House, 1982), pp. 32–33.

Ch. 5 God revives his people

1 Cited in Erroll Hulse, *Give Him No Rest* (Darlington: Evangelical Press, 1991), pp. 61–62.

2 Edwards, *Revival!*, pp. 271–275.

3 Jonathan Edwards, *The Works of Jonathan Edwards*, vol. i (Edinburgh: Banner of Truth, 1974), p. 539.

4 D. Martyn Lloyd-Jones, *Revival* (Westchester, IL: Crossway, 1987), p. 163.

ABOUT DAY ONE:

Day One's threefold commitment:
- • To be faithful to the Bible, God's inerrant, infallible Word;
- • To be relevant to our modern generation;
- • To be excellent in our publication standards.

I continue to be thankful for the publications of Day One. They are biblical; they have sound theology; and they are relevant to the issues at hand. The material is condensed and manageable while, at the same time, being complete—a challenging balance to find. We are happy in our ministry to make use of these excellent publications.

JOHN MACARTHUR, PASTOR-TEACHER, GRACE COMMUNITY CHURCH, CALIFORNIA

It is a great encouragement to see Day One making such excellent progress. Their publications are always biblical, accessible and attractively produced, with no compromise on quality. Long may their progress continue and increase!

JOHN BLANCHARD, AUTHOR, EVANGELIST AND APOLOGIST

Visit our web site for more information and
to request a free catalogue of our books.

www.dayone.co.uk

U.S. web site:
www.dayonebookstore.com

5 Hulse, *Give Him No Rest*, pp. 108–109.

6 Gordon Keddie, *Dawn of a Kingdom* (Welwyn: Evangelical Press, 1988), p. 80.

Ch. 7 God's people are humbled

1 Albert Barnes, *Barnes' Notes: Isaiah* (Grand Rapids, MI: Baker, 2005), p. 139.

Ch. 8 God's people pray

1 Edwards, *Works*, vol. i, p. 426.

2 Ibid.

Ch. 9 God's people repent

1 Edwards, *Revival!*, p. 114.

Ch. 10 God's people value God's Word

1 Cited by John MacArthur, 'Preaching the Word in and out of Season', 2000, at: biblebb.com.

Ch. 11 God's people prize his house and his gospel

1 Roger Ellsworth, *They Echoed the Voice of God: Reflections on the Minor Prophets* (Leominster: Day One, 2008), p. 24.

2 Edwards, *Revival!*, p. 42.

3 Ibid. p. 122.

Ch. 13 The hopeful plea of a hopeful heart

1 James Montgomery Boice, *Psalms*, vol. ii (Grand Rapids, MI: Baker, 1996), p. 744.